Pre-Discipleship

The Forgotten Element in Evangelism

Kai Mark

PRE-DISCIPLESHIP
The Forgotten Element in Evangelism

ISBN-10: 1-897373-94-5
ISBN-13: 978-1897373-94-1

Printed by Word Alive Press
131 Cordite Road, Winnipeg, MB R3W 1S1
www.wordalivepress.ca

WORD ALIVE PRESS
Just Write!

Printed in Canada.

Acknowledgements

I want to first thank the Lord for His wisdom and grace in the writing of this book. I want to thank my family: my wife Margaret, my son Gregory, and my daughter Lindsay, for their patience all these years I've wrestled with the issues of evangelism. I also want to thank the leaders of Unionville Oasis Church, who encouraged me on this journey to the end.

Foreword

I was with Franklin Graham at a MissionFest in Toronto in 1996, thirteen years ago when I first met Kai. Shortly after that I had a stroke after many years of ministry as an evangelist. It was when I was recovering from the stroke that I began to know Kai. Since then, I had written a book about having a stroke called *Suddenly Silenced*. Kai's grandmother also had a stroke when she was about 90 years old, and yet she continued to serve the Lord. After our first encounter at that MissionFest, Kai and I began to meet on a monthly basis at my house for fellowship and encouragement.

Kai was one of the pastors at Richmond Hill Chinese Community Church, where I preached at least two times. It was at Kai's church that I first preached after my stroke. Kai is a graduate of Liberty University and received his Master of Divinity at Tyndale Seminary, close to where I live and where my son Wesley was dedicated. Kai recently received his Doctor of Ministry from Gordon-Conwell Theological Seminary and we continue to enjoy blessed fellowship together.

This book that Kai wrote is about a forgotten aspect in evangelism. Today many Christians forget to realize that our goal in evangelism is to make disciples of Jesus Christ. Many evangelistic efforts have resulted in decisions for Christ, but there have been very few disciples. Kai gives us a fresh way of looking at evangelism. I would encourage everyone to read this book as it helps us rethink some important aspects in the way we share the good news of Jesus.

Dr. John Wesley White

Introduction

My journey in reflection on the gospel began when my former pastor, the late Rev. Martin Wedge, admitted to me that our denomination was dying. At that time in the late eighties, I was a young pastor and he was ministering in the head office of the denomination. I was in shock from his statement. I grew up being told that our denomination had all the right theology and practices. It did bother me that some leaders in my denomination looked down on other denominations, but I never expected that our pride and arrogance would result in the tangible decline in our denominational community.

This experience forced me to reflect on the gospel that we were preaching. I reasoned that our dying churches were either due to the possibility that the gospel has no power to transform lives, as we would like it to have, or that we are not preaching the life-changing gospel. I found it difficult to believe that the gospel is powerless. God is real and my experiences with Him have revealed that the gospel does change lives, including mine. I concluded that we, evangelicals, are not preaching the life-changing message of the gospel. I discovered that many times evangelicals preach a message without an emphasis on repentance. I have seen preachers who manipulate people to acknowledge Christ, pray a sinner's prayer, and even join a local church, even though the people have very little understanding of repentance. I have also discovered that evangelicals are very good at getting people to believe in Jesus, but this often does not result in people following Jesus. Imagine that, a gospel that does not result in repentance or discipleship.

It was through this journey that I began to understand that Jesus wanted us to repent, to believe in Him, and to follow Him in order to be His disciples. Many of our gospel presentations end with the encouragement for seekers to accept Christ, when Jesus wants us to do more than just accept Him. He wants us to repent of our sins, believe in Him, and be willing to follow Him.

I feel passionate about this because the bottom line is that we are not producing disciples. Our efforts, energies, finances, and prayers result in very few disciples. This can be very discouraging, until we understand two things. First, the biblical gospel is life-changing and has the power to transform lives. Second, the way people become disciples of Jesus in the New Testament is very different from the way people become disciples today. Seekers in the New Testament examined the Scriptures and had a foundational understanding of the Word of God before they became children of God. However, we encourage many seekers today to come to Christ without any basic understanding of Jesus or Christianity.

Jesus never wanted anyone to follow him with little or no understanding. He told the crowd following him, *"If anyone would come after me, he must deny himself and take up his cross and follow me"* (Mark 8:34b). In other words, if you want to follow me, you must give up yourself and be prepared to die. Jesus told his potential disciples to consider the cost of following him. It is like a person who is building a tower; he must first consider the costs or he will not complete what he started to build. Jesus also wants his prospective disciples to understand and know what it means to follow him. It is like a king who is about to go to war and evaluates his situation before heading into battle. Jesus said, *"In the same way, any of you who does not give up everything he has cannot be my disciples"* (Luke 14:33). Jesus never encouraged people to follow him without realizing their level of commitment.

This book is the result of these years of struggle in understanding evangelism. Hopefully it will help the church to rethink preaching the good news biblically, theologically, socially, historically, and practically. I pray that it will inspire and motivate readers to think in ways that will impact eternity. Wisdom tells us, *"It is a trap for a man to dedicate something rashly and only later to consider his vows"* (Proverbs 20:25). The Lord never wanted anyone to rashly follow him. Let us begin to learn to bring many to Him through a pre-discipleship process that has been forgotten!

Table of Contents

CHAPTER ONE:
OUR PROBLEMS IN EVANGELISM

"Therefore go and make disciples of all nations, baptizing them in the name of the Father and of the Son and of the Holy Spirit, and teaching them to obey everything I have commanded you. And surely I am with you always, to the very end of the age" (Matthew 28:19-20).

Since the days of the early church, Christians have encountered difficulties in meeting this challenge to share their faith and make disciples. The early church believers faced persecution and death, while many missionaries have dealt with hardships. In the past century, the church has engaged in many evangelistic and missionary efforts, but it seems that these endeavours have had limited effectiveness in enabling new believers to become disciples (committed followers) of Christ.

My own journey in evangelism and discipleship started as a young teen at a Christian youth retreat where I was challenged with the command that Christians must share their faith. I began wearing "Jesus buttons" in high school and handed comic-style tracts out to my classmates. My thrill that year was leading a classmate in the salvation after going through The Four Spiritual Laws with him. By the time I was eighteen, I had engaged in door-to-door evangelism in two communities, sharing the gospel with whoever would listen. In spite of being an introvert, I witnessed for Jesus and he used me through the years to lead hundreds to him through the practice of preaching, teaching, and personal witnessing.

Yet something troubled me. It seemed that only a few of those who had come to Christ through my ministry were continuing as disciples of Christ. That's when I realized that many ministries had the same problem. Although Christians spend much money, time, and energy to reach the lost, the number of disciples produced seems to be far fewer than the number of converts. This left me with many questions about the methods used to share the gospel of Jesus Christ and about how I could evangelize in such a way that more converts became disciples. Those questions led to an investigation of evangelism and discipleship, which eventually laid the foundation for this book.

My experiences in evangelism made me realize that we Christians have shown little creativity in our evangelistic efforts and have settled for using the same old methods that have relatively little effect. However, these are not the only problems associated with evangelism today. Others include a lack of concern for evangelism, a lack of a positive image for evangelism, a lack of pure faith, a lack of cultural relevance, and a lack of disciples. The exploration of these problems is necessary because learning how to become more effective in making disciples out of converts begins with understanding what is causing churches to fail at it. Identifying the problems with evangelism will enable Christians to focus on the issues that need to be addressed and then understand which solutions might be effective.

LACK OF CONCERN FOR EVANGELISM

My evangelistic experiences have left me feeling that evangelism is not a top priority among Christians. We love to attend conferences on worship, discipleship, and leadership, but we are not as enthusiastic about reaching the lost. We know that evangelism is one of the things we ought to do in our Christian walk, but the majority of believers in North America have very little idea of how to do this well. The lack of success in past attempts for outreach reinforces in the minds of many Christians that they are not cut out for evangelism.

The lack of concern for achieving effective evangelism in many North American churches arises from a number of factors, including confusion about the nature of evangelism, pluralism, and poor values.

A misunderstanding of evangelism has influenced some Christians to think that they are witnessing simply by letting others know that they are Christians. The tolerant context in society makes some Christians uncomfortable with personally sharing the gospel with others lest they seem intrusive. Richard Winter, in commenting about people's boredom in a culture of entertainment, writes, "When everything is allowed in the name of tolerance, then there is nothing worth standing for, and as a result the soul begins to wither and die. A sense of apathy and disengagement from life takes over. A feeling that everything is tedious and annoying underlies all thoughts."[1]

Many North American Christians have misplaced values and priorities that seem to have affected their attitudes toward evangelism. Most churchgoers are so busy with work, family, and social commitments that they do not have much time for God, ministry, and evangelism. Ron Hutchcraft writes, "And the busier we get, the more self-absorbed we are. We are so preoccupied with our responsibilities, our fatigue, and our unfinished work that we can't seem to fit anyone else in! When life overheats, children become intruders, co-workers are a nuisance, and every other driver is in the way."[2]

Christians in general are apathetic when it comes to evangelism. However, for those who do care, we have become too busy to be concerned with the destiny of the lost. Our preoccupation with our high-paced lives has left us with very little time to share our faith. The lives of North American Christians are saturated with many aimless commitments. We have reduced evangelism to a program one signs up for rather than a way of life.

LACK OF A POSITIVE IMAGE OF EVANGELISM

A Christian leader once joked with me that the one thing that Christians and non-Christians have in common is that they both hate evangelism.

---

[1] Richard Winter, *Still Bored In A Culture of Entertainment: Rediscovering Passion and Wonder* (Downers Grove, IL: InterVarsity Press, 2002), 92.
[2] Ron Hutchcraft, *Living Peacefully in a Stressful World: A Strategy for Replacing Stress with Peace* (Grand Rapids, MI: Discovery House Publishers, 2000), 115.

When believers are challenged to engage in evangelism, they have been trained to build up relationships with non-believers in order to look for opportunities to present a prescript gospel presentation, which hopefully result in prayers for salvation. The practice of evangelism has become something that is unnatural and uncomfortable to many Christians.

The poor image of evangelism in society, and in some churches, may deter a number of Christians from engaging in outreach. Some Christians have been taught to be aggressive and even obnoxious when it comes to sharing the gospel, in the belief that the end justifies the means. Michael Simpson, a strategist on evangelism writes,

> Evangelism as most people know it is an unnatural act. Christians knock on stranger's doors, interrupting their time with their family, stop random people in the street, divert vacationers' enjoyment, and flash Bible verses at sporting events. Others stand on street corners spouting the promise of eternal damnation at passersby with a white-knuckled grip on a well-worn Bible, which appears more as a weapon than a beacon of hope.[3]

Simpson compared the methods of some evangelicals to annoying telemarketers pushing their products onto uninformed and unwilling strangers, robbing victims of their time with interruptions. Simpson writes, "I don't think it is likely that anyone in a westernized country will accept Christ after being randomly stopped on a busy street for a night on the town. I do, however personally know of hundreds of people that have been loved into salvation."[4]

The image of evangelism has also been tarnished by the reduction of evangelism into a pre-packaged sales pitch given to unsuspecting strangers with the intent of closing the sale. Renowned Canadian author

---

[3] Michael L. Simpson, *Permission Evangelism: When to Talk, When to Walk* (Paris, ON: NexGen, 2003), 15.
[4] Ibid, 14.

Margaret Atwood compared evangelism to indecent exposure in a story featuring Christine, who was raised an Anglican and, while on a journey to Florida, met a woman who told her that she used to be a missionary. Atwood describes Christine's reaction:

> Religious people of any serious kind made her nervous: they were like men in raincoats who might or might not be flashers. You would be going along with them in the normal way, and then there could be a swift movement and you would look down to find the coat wide open and nothing on under it but some pant legs held up by the rubber bands. This had happened to Christine in a train station once.[5]

Indecent exposure is a criminal offense. Flashers act inappropriately, and cheapen what should be kept private. The expression of intimacy becomes a means of intimidating the victim. In response to Atwood, John Bowen writes, "So this is how one of Canada's most articulate and sensitive writers views evangelism: it is dehumanizing, violent, and inappropriate. These are strong words. No wonder many Christians back away from the 'E' word. We have no desire to be spiritual flashers. We just don't want to be seen that way."[6] With the image of evangelism in such a battered state, it is imperative that we rethink the way Jesus Christ is presented.

LACK OF A PURE FAITH

Another problem we face in evangelism is syncretism. Syncretism is the reconciliation of different beliefs. It creates problems in evangelism because it produces followers who lack true faith. In some cases, people have mixed pagan or heretical beliefs with their new Christian beliefs, as John Cross discusses:

---

[5] Margaret Atwood, *Bluebeard's Egg* (Toronto: McCelland and Stewart, 1984), 169.
[6] John P. Bowen, *Evangelism For "Normal" People: Good News for Those Looking for a Fresh Approach* (Minneapolis, MN: Augsburg Fortress, 2002), 19–20.

> Syncretism is a huge problem in missions. This is not an exaggeration. For example, in some places in the world, it is reported that vast numbers of people have converted to Christianity ... Are these conversions no more than paper statistics? Well, I would be loathe to accuse anyone of falsifying records, but I think we can safely say that time has proven that a significant number of these "converts" are highly syncretized "believers." Some consider these folk "Christians" whereas others say that there is *no way* they can be "saved."[7]

Syncretism, which is regarded as common in foreign cultures, is an unrecognized problem in North America. Many North American converts to Christianity have integrated the Christian faith into their non-biblical understanding of life. They may agree with the basics precepts of Christian theology in terms of God, Jesus, and the Bible, but still act on their superstitions, such as continuing to follow their horoscope. It would not be surprising to find many who claim to have embraced Christ without having rejected their New Age practices. Dave Hunt and T.A. McMahon reported "in Hollywood, California, in an occult bookstore, a pair of teenage girls, whose parents take them each Sunday to fundamentalist Christian churches, browse through the parentally forbidden shelves on witchcraft, eager to discover for themselves the promised powers."[8]

The rivalry for allegiance between Christianity and paganism that is expressed in the worship of idols or ancestors in some cultures, takes a different form in North America. Here time, money, status, education, and health are as highly exalted as the Lord God. Many Christian boards often first make "business decisions," and then come to the Lord for his stamp of approval. Some Christian leaders have treated people

---

[7] John R. Cross, *And Beginning With Moses: Teaching Those Who Know Little or Nothing about the Bible* (Olds, AB: Goodseed International, 2002), 11–12.
[8] Dave Hunt and T.A. McMahon, *America: The Sorcerer's New Apprentice* (Eugene, OR: Harvest House Publishers, 1988), 274.

with money, status, or education differently than they should. Many in North American churches who profess Christ are, in practice, atheists, agnostic, or pagan, when, for example, they do not seriously pray or seek God when making major decisions.

LACK OF CULTURAL RELEVANCE

A fourth problem with evangelism, and one related to the issue of syncretism, is the lack of relevance of evangelism in today's postmodern world. Postmodernists reject the metanarratives in modernity, including those in Christianity, and embrace a plurality of truths, making traditional Christian approaches to evangelism irrelevant. Postmodernists accept the legitimacy of all beliefs, of which Christianity is one. In his analysis of postmodernism, Stanley Grenz states:

> In a sense, postmoderns have no worldview. A denial of the reality of a unified world as the object of our perception is at the heart of postmodernism. Postmoderns reject the possibility of constructing a single correct worldview and are content simply to speak of many views and by extension, many worlds.
>
> By replacing the modern worldview with a multiplicity of views and worlds, the postmodern era has in effect replaced knowledge with interpretation.[9]

Postmodernists view truth as being relative and do not accept that there are absolute truths, such as those claimed by Christianity "The diversity of religious and philosophical perspectives available to people today makes the notion of one absolutely true religion or philosophy unacceptable."[10] The difference of paradigms in understanding truth means that the modern methods of evangelism may not be as effective

---

[9] Stanley J. Grenz, *A Primer On Postmodernism* (Grand Rapids, MI: William B. Eerdmans Publishing, 1996), 40.
[10] Douglas Groothuis, *Truth Decay: Defending Christianity Against the Challenges of Postmodernism* (Downers Grove, IL: InterVarsity Press, 2000), 28.

as in the past. Gene Veith writes about the difficulty in sharing the truth with "people who believe that true is relative ('Jesus works for you; crystals work for her'). It is hard to proclaim the forgiveness of sins to people who believe that, since morality is relative, they have no sins to forgive."[11]

Postmodernists in North America no longer embrace the Christian worldview or even have a biblical understanding of the cosmos. As a result, models like *Evangelism Explosion, The Four Spiritual Laws,* and *Alpha*, which were developed in a time when unbelievers still had some biblical background, are no longer as effective as they were. Postmodernists need to be reached through new models of evangelism. Grenz concludes his study on postmodernism, saying,

> We dare not simply "move with the times" and embrace uncritically the latest intellectual trend. At the same time, critical engagement with postmodern-ism cannot end with a simplistic rejection of the entire ethos. Our critical reflections must lead us to determine the contours of the gospel that will speak to the hearts of postmodern people. We must engage postmodernism in order to discern how best to articulate the Christian faith to the next generation.[12]

LACK OF DISCIPLES

A fifth and major problem in evangelism is that many of the existing approaches have been rather ineffective in producing disciples, the reason for which Christians practice evangelism. The data shows that the ratio of disciples to those who have been evangelized is low.

Robert Coleman in *The Master Plan of Evangelism*, first published in 1963, describes one popular strategy that the Christian community adopted. Coleman suggested using a process of selection, association,

---

[11] Gene Edward Veith Jr., *Postmodern Times: A Christian Guide to Contemporary Thought and Culture* (Wheaton, IL: Crossway Books, 1994), 16.

[12] Grenz, 174.

consecration, impartation, demonstration, delegation, supervision, and reproduction to evangelize the world. He uses Jesus as the model evangelist and states, "Everything He did and said was a part of the whole pattern. It had significance because it contributed to the ultimate purpose of His life in redeeming the world for God."[13] Coleman's model was significant in that his understanding of evangelism was not limited to it merely preaching the gospel, but also to being a process and lifestyle that brought people into discipleship.

In the past century, numerous evangelistic meetings, campaigns, and crusades have been conducted that boast numbers of converts in the thousands and hundreds of thousands. The Billy Graham Evangelistic Association (BGEA), for example, has reported that in 2005 about 3.2 million people confessed Jesus as Lord. One BGEA report says, "As we proclaimed the Gospel around the world, the Holy Spirit swept through downcast hearts, and we know of 3.2 million people who bowed before their Savior Jesus Christ. Only eternity will reveal the full harvest of 2005."[14] However, after many evangelistic campaigns, local pastors and Christians leaders found that only a handful of the thousands reached had become disciples who were committed to Jesus Christ.

Win Arn, a church growth consultant who conducted a follow up study on the 1976 Billy Graham Crusade in Seattle, found that the crusade was not effective in producing disciples. *Decision* magazine claimed that the Seattle campaign was the "most exciting and successful U.S. Billy Graham Crusade in years."[15] About 434,100 attended the crusade and 18,136 people made some kind of decision for Christ. Arn found that only fifteen percent of those who professed Christ had been incorporated into a church. He pointed out that, of the 434,100 who attended the crusade, only 0.29 percent became new

---

[13] Robert E. Coleman, *The Master Plan of Evangelism* (Old Tappan, NJ: Fleming H. Revell Company, 1973), 13.
[14] Billy Graham Evangelistic Association. Annual Report, 2005 fiscal year, 3. http://www.billygraham.org/pdfs/development/annualreports/BGEA2005AnnualReport.pdf, accessed October 23, 2008.
[15] Sherwood E. Wirt, "Rescue for Seattle," *Decision* (August 1976), 8.

members of a church,[16] and concluded that there must be more effective ways of engaging in evangelism.

Campus Crusade for Christ launched a major evangelistic effort in 1976 in partnership with local churches. In the United States and Canada, more than 265 major metropolitan cities participated in this campaign and they produced seemingly successful results. The Christian leaders at that time were determined not to repeat the ineffective saturation evangelistic programs used a decade earlier. They were optimistic about the outcome because they were making a creative and collective use of the media in presenting the gospel and this was the first time a para-church organization was collaborating with a number of local churches.

Afterwards, research was conducted in six test cities to evaluate the impact of the campaign. "The following data were collected from 178 churches in the six test cities: 26,535 gospel presentations, 4,106 decisions for Christ, 526 in Bible studies led by church members, and 125 new church members. In other words, of the 4,106 people who made decisions, three percent became church members"[17] and less than half a percent (0.47 percent) of those who heard the gospel presentations became church members. In reality fewer than that would have become committed disciples of Christ. Christians have spent millions of dollars and an enormous amount of time and energy, resulting in only a few disciples.

The above statistics assumed that church membership could be equated with maturity in Christ. However, church membership is only an indicator of discipleship and does not equate to discipleship. One can assume that every disciple of Jesus will become a church member, but must acknowledge that not all church members are growing disciples of Christ. As well, just because a North American church has growing attendance numbers, it does not mean that the church is making disciples, since growth may be influenced by other factors such as biological growth, the meeting of social needs in the community,

---

[16] Win Arn, "Mass Evangelism: The Bottom Line," *Church Growth: America* 4, no. 1 (1978), 7.
[17] Peter Wagner, "Who Found It?" *EternityMagazine* (September 1977), 16.

clever marketing, or the attractiveness of programs. This does not mean North American churches should cease their functioning programs, though they should critically analyze whether or not disciples are being made.

Much of the failure to produce disciples in evangelism can be attributed to the lack of follow-up, a situation that occurs because many Christians understand evangelism and discipleship to be separate functions, whereas Scripture sees them as one. The church's lack of follow-up or attempts to educate converts before or after they prayed the "sinner's prayer" have led to weak and often harmful conversions. Some people who thought they were saved because they had said a prayer are actually not, because they do not have a genuine personal relationship with Jesus Christ. Ray Comfort comments on these weak conversions when he writes, "If you want decisions, I can get them. But if you want to see people 'saved,' that's different—salvation is of the Lord."[18]

The cry for follow-up by church leaders is another indicator that some gospel presentations are inadequate. Many critics point to the "lack of follow-up" as the reason so many evangelistic efforts have failed. The very existence of follow-up is an admission that somehow our delivery of the good news is not good enough. The result of many decisions for Christ compared to the number of disciples for Christ should alarm every Christian who has a passion for soul-winning.

The problems in evangelism in today's church are numerous. The five problems mentioned are only glimpses of the chaotic state of our outreach to the lost world. The purpose of this book is not to identify all the problems in evangelism but to come to a biblical solution to some of our problems. The majority of the problems in evangelism can be summed up in the "thousand to one" reality.

---

[18] Ray Comfort, *Hell's Best Kept Secret* (New Kensington, PA: Whitaker House, 1989), 67.

CHAPTER TWO:

THE NEED FOR PRE-DISCIPLESHIP

If I ask you me whether or not a thousand to one are good odds, you may say, "That depends!" If we are talking about a game of chance, they are better odds than a one in a million. If we are talking about the odds of recovering from a disease, the sick person faces a very grim future. If I told you that for every thousand people we share the gospel with, we produce one disciple, you may acknowledge that those are extremely poor odds. If all of our efforts, money, resources, and energies in reaching the lost are producing disciples at ratio of a thousand to one, it is time to begin rethinking our evangelistic strategies.

Consider the statistics from the Seattle Billy Graham Crusade in 1976, mentioned in the previous chapter. Remember that this was the "most exciting and successful U.S. Billy Graham Crusade in years."[19] That means the numbers for success in this crusade were high, higher than most efforts in evangelism. In the end, being statistically one of the most successful crusades, the result was that only 0.29 percent of those who were at the crusade became new church members. This means that if only one thousand people attended the crusade, only three people would become church members.

One must not assume that church members equates to being disciples of Christ. It is highly likely that a disciple of Christ will become a church member, but not all church members are disciples of Christ. Not all church members have made a conscious effort to follow Jesus. Many church members who are very religious in nature have a

---

[19] Sherwood E. Wirt, "Rescue for Seattle," *Decision* (August 1976), 8.

form of godliness, but are more lovers of themselves, money, and pleasure than lovers of God. They are boastful, proud, abusive, disobedient to their parents, ungrateful, unholy, without love, without self-control, unforgiving, slanderous, brutal, treacherous, rash, and conceited.

According to the data cited, less than five percent of those who hear the gospel make decisions for Christ. The studies also show that only about three to ten percent of the less than five percent who make decisions become church members. Richard Peace supports the higher end of the range: "statistics indicate that on average only ten percent of those who respond at an evangelistic meeting become active disciples of Jesus."[20] The studies mentioned earlier in this book revealed that the range of three to ten percent varies, depending on the length of time that passes between the study and the campaign, and the amount of personal follow-up that occurs with the converts. If a thousand people heard the gospel through an evangelistic effort, less than five percent, or fifty people, would have made decisions for Christ. Since five percent is on the high end for even a successful evangelistic campaign, it may be more realistic to suggest a number less than five percent to be a normal response to the gospel.

For argument's sake, let us say that two-thirds of that five percent is the normal response to the gospel. This would mean that for every thousand people who hear the gospel, there may be an average of thirty-three decisions for Christ. Out of those who make decisions for Christ, only about three to ten percent become church members, which means that for every thousand people who hear the gospel, only one to three people eventually become church members. Although one can assume that every disciple of Christ today is committed to the local church, one cannot make the same assumption that every church member is a committed disciple of Christ. The number of disciples will certainly be less than the number of church members. However, through the studies given, it is logical to state that for every disciple

---

[20] Richard V. Peace, *Conversion in the New Testament: Paul and the Twelve* (Grand Rapids, MI: Wm B. Eerdmans Publishing Company, 1999), 305.

that is made, the church today must statistically share the gospel with more than a thousand people.

THE CONTEXT FOR PRE-DISCIPLESHIP

The thousand to one scenario reinforces the need for an alternative approach to evangelism. Some have attributed the successes and failures of evangelism to the quantity and quality of planning, prayer, follow-up, and church involvement, and to the level of involvement of the Holy Spirit. However, other factors also contribute to the outcome of an evangelistic effort, such as the repeated use of approaches and strategies that have not succeeded and do not address changes in worldview. There is a need for an evangelism strategy that engages Christians unashamedly in a natural way with the postmodern community and enables the church to become effective in making disciples.

A few years ago, I planted a church in the city of Markham in Ontario, Canada. A Buddhist family visited our church. They asked if they could continue to come and attend our church even though they were Buddhists. I told them that they were always welcome, and eventually had an opportunity to share the gospel with the family. Their response to the gospel was that they were not yet ready to embrace Christianity fully, but they would still appreciate it if they could attend our church. What can we do for those who have heard the gospel, but do not feel they are ready to make such a serious commitment to Jesus?

They, like many others today, did not have a background for understanding Christianity and had no opportunity to learn about the faith. What do we do with those who have heard the gospel but are not yet ready to totally trust in Jesus? There is a need for pre-discipleship, a process of introducing people to the Bible and Christian beliefs before expecting them to make any major commitments. Pre-discipleship was a common biblical practice that is rarely practiced today. A Google search in April 2007 for "pre-discipleship" revealed that less than forty websites contained the word. Many of the organizations that produced these sites use pre-discipleship as a pre-study tool for new believers to prepare them to move fully into discipleship. Others use pre-discipleship as a kind of discipleship for children, but only a few sites indicated ministries that used pre-discipleship as a process of evangelism. However, in just over a year and a half later, October 2008, there were about two hundred Christian websites that contained the word "pre-discipleship," with about one tenth of those sites using the word as a process of evangelism.

THE EXISTENCE OF PRE-DISCIPLESHIP

There is a need and a place for Christians to provide context to seekers for understanding Christianity before they are put face to face with the heart of the gospel. In this book, *pre-discipleship is defined as a process of evangelism that engages seekers in a study of the Word of God to the point that they are able make a commitment—intellectually, emotionally, and volitionally—as to whether they will or will not follow Jesus.* It is the process that Trevor McIlwain, a New Tribes missionary working with the Palawano people in the Philippines, called building a foundation for the gospel. He said that evangelicals make the mistake of presenting peoples' needs when sharing the gospel, and then quickly turning to the remedy of Christ without spending sufficient time preparing those people for the gospel.

> Because Western society has a facade of Christianity, most Christian workers presume that people already have the foundations of the Gospel. We assume they already have a basic understanding of God and His nature and character. However, the vast majority of people in so-called Christian countries have little biblical knowledge of God. Of the relatively few in our countries who do attend church, most have a humanistic and unscriptural concept of God.[21]

McIlwain developed a pre-discipleship approach after discovering that, although many people in his ministry had been Christianized, they

---

[21] Trevor McIlwain, *Firm Foundations: Creations to Christ* (Sanford, FL: New Tribes Mission, 1993), 28.

were not Christians. Because of his struggle to correct the impact of syncretism, McIlwain developed *Firm Foundations*, a series of fifty lessons that taught the foundations of Christianity so a person could understand the gospel fully. The lessons taught the Scriptures from creation to Christ through the use of story.

> His-story, that is, the story of Christ, begins in the first verse of Genesis, for He was there in the beginning. But it is not until the fall of man that the Son of the virgin is promised, One who will overcome Satan and deliver his captives. The story of Christ then continues through the entire Old Testament in numerous types and prophecies. The New Testament records the fulfillment of these prophecies through His birth, life, death, ascension, and present glory. The story of Christ as told in the Gospels is the sequel to the Old Testament.[22]

Since the 1980s, New Tribes Mission has continued to develop this storytelling approach to the Bible, finding that it aided tribal people in digesting the truths of the Bible and the gospel. John Cross of Goodseed International describes the value of this method: "Since tribal people know nothing of the Bible, this approach by necessity addressed those issues that exist in a biblically-illiterate society. This format of Bible teaching was found to be extremely effective in countering the confusion that results in syncretism and reaching those ignorant of the Bible."[23]

Cross adopted this method of evangelism, and in *The Stranger on the Road to Emmaus*, which was first printed in 1996, he encourages seekers to first get the overview of the Bible and then to go back to discover the details. Cross writes, "Get the big picture first ... once you

---

[22] Ibid., 32.
[23]. Cross, *And Beginning with Moses*, 22.

have the big picture in mind, you can go back and fill in the details by getting your questions answered."[24]

Another attempt at pre-discipleship is the Alpha Course, developed in England in 1977 by Nicky Gumbel, an Anglican priest, for Anglicans. The approach recognized that evangelism involves a process of study and of gaining understanding over time. "The Alpha course consists of a series of talks addressing key issues relating to the Christian faith."[25] Alpha is delivered over fifteen weeks through videos and small group discussions after people have shared a meal, but the lessons can be covered in ten weeks along with a weekend retreat. The topics covered range from the relevancy of Christianity to Jesus, the Holy Spirit, healing, and the church today. In his *Questions of Life*, Gumbel writes, "This book attempts to answer some of the key questions at the heart of the Christian faith."[26] The Alpha Course has been very popular, and Alpha International's official website claims that more than eight million people have taken the course in thirty different countries around the world, bringing many people to Christ.[27]

Alpha uses a personal approach that is appropriate in evangelism in a post-Christian society. Stephen Hunt, a critic of Alpha, writes,

> Evangelism had therefore come to require a totally new direction—a more personal one. Moreover, it had to present a soft, not a hard sell. Put more directly, a fresh approach to evangelism, typified by *Alpha,* needed to be one which was user-friendly. There was no room for "in your face," repent or to hell with you, obtrusive Christianity.[28]

---

[24] John R. Cross, *The Stranger on the Road to Emmaus Workbook* (Durham, ON: Goodseed International, 2000), 7.

[25] Alpha International, *The Alpha Course.* http://alpha.org/itv/whatisit, Accessed 18 September 2006.

[26] Nicky Gumbel, *Questions of Life: A Practical Introduction to the Christian Faith* (Eastbourne, E. Sussex: Kingsway Publications, 1995), 9.

[27] Alpha International, *The Alpha Course*, http://alpha.org/default.asp, Accessed 15 August 2007.

[28] Stephen Hunt, *Anyone For Alpha?: Inside a Leading Evangelising Initiative* (London: Darton, Longman and Todd Ltd., 2001), 10-11.

The success resulting from *Firm Foundations*, *The Stranger on the Road to Emmaus*, and *Alpha* reinforced the importance and validity of using some form of pre-discipleship in evangelism. While *Firm Foundations* and *The Stranger on the Road* are helpful tools, it can be impractical to expect a seeker to spend fifty, or even fifteen, weeks studying Christianity. It is much easier in the busyness of modern life to get a commitment with a seeker to meet for a shorter time, such as six or seven weeks.

One drawback to the Alpha Course is that while it appeals to seekers who have had former church experience, it might not appeal to seekers who have no Christian background. Topics like "How can I be filled with the Spirit?" would not appeal to those who had no exposure to Christianity. There is a hunger for tools that introduce Christ to those who have no concept or background in Christianity, tools that will assist a seeker in the pre-discipleship process.

While some may dismiss pre-discipleship as simply another method of evangelism, it is a necessary process in reaching the world for Christ. It is necessary because it communicates the gospel in a way that results in a clear understanding of the salvation message. John Cross emphasizes the importance of a pre-discipleship when he writes,

> In communicating a message, the methods are seemingly endless. By method we are not referring to the *means*, which could range from the spoken word to smoke signals and drums. Rather we are talking about *how* the message is arranged in the process of passing it on. For example what is its emphasis? Is the message communicated topically, word by word, as a narrative, systematically, or by "leaping around?" All of these are dynamics that define a method—or lack of a method.[29]

---

[29] Cross, *And Beginning with Moses*, 25.

THE CRY FOR PRE-DISCIPLESHIP

Pre-discipleship comes from the need for seekers of Christianity to be well informed of all the implications of making a commitment to Christ. Most people who hear the gospel for the first time do not make a commitment to Jesus Christ. Very few seek God in a spiritual journey and begin to embrace Jesus after hearing the gospel. An example of this is the Ethiopian eunuch who was on the road out of Jerusalem. He was already searching and reading the book of Isaiah when he first heard the gospel from Philip, and was quickly baptized. The majority of people who hear the gospel for the first time need time to digest the Word of God. This is a natural reaction to the gospel. After all, if making a commitment to Jesus Christ is the most important relationship in one's life, how can we expect people to make such a commitment to Him without going through any kind of courtship?

The accounts of some of the Athenians' responses to hearing the gospel provide insight concerning how people initially respond to the gospel. When the Apostle Paul spoke on Mars Hill in Athens, it was the first time many Athenians heard the gospel. They had three different, yet classic, types of responses to it. One group rejected the gospel: *"some of them sneered"* (Acts 17:32) after hearing about the resurrection of the dead. Some in the audience reserved judgment: *"We want to hear you again on this subject"* (Acts 17:32). Others were receptive: *"A few men became followers of Paul and believed"* (Acts 17:34). These are three common responses of those who hear the gospel for the first time: they reject the gospel, they reserve the right to hear more about it, or they receive and embrace the gospel.

Many commentators describe Paul's experience in Athens as a "you win some, you lose some" situation.

> Was Paul's ministry in Athens successful? The ans-
> wer to this question could be yes or it could be no,
> depending on our understanding of Paul's goals. If
> we understand that his goal was to deliver a speech
> that was theologically impeccable and yet skillfully
> contextualized to the culture of Greek philosophers,

we would say he was successful. Many students of
Paul consider his address on Mars Hill as the finest of
all his recorded speeches. If we understand Paul's
goal as winning a debate with the sophisticated
intellectuals of what could be seen as Harvard of the
first century, we would say that he failed. And if we
understand that, more likely, his primary goal was to
win people to Christ and to plant a strong church in
Athens, Paul definitely was much less than successful.[30]

Pre-discipleship is a process for those who want to hear more.
However, most commentators do not pay attention to them and group
them with the mockers, failing to understand that many people, like
those Athenians, need more time and information before accepting or
rejecting Jesus. It is wrong to expect all people to make a sound
commitment to Jesus when they first encounter the gospel. Some will,
but most will not.

Statistically, the number of people that embrace the gospel when
they first hear it is small. "Less than five percent of those who respond
to an altar call during a public crusade ... are living a Christian life one
year later."[31] Those who respond positively have often been prepared in
their hearts by God, either through some form of pre-discipleship or a
dramatic experience. Others respond because they are at a stage in life
where they will respond to almost anything, but do not respond to
Christ because they do not have a total understanding of the gospel.

At the same time, few reject the gospel outright when they first
hear it. Ipsos-Reid polls show that only one in ten Canadians say they
do not believe in God.[32] After all, most people do not have enough
information to reject Jesus intelligently after hearing the gospel for the
first time in a limited presentation. They may reject the inconvenience,
or the way one presents the gospel. Some may even reject the present-

---

[30] C. Peter Wagner, *Acts of the Holy Spirit* (Ventura, CA: Regal Books, 2000), 436.

[31] Ray Comfort, "Alarming Statistics," www.livingwaters.com/pastor.shtml, accessed
October 24, 2008.

[32] www.ipsos-na.com/news/pressrelease.cfm?id=1957, accessed October 24, 2008.

ation of the gospel out of ignorance and fear because of their belief system. However, very few, if any, seekers of truth will outright reject the gospel after being confronted with it for the first time.

If a small percentage of people reject the gospel and another five percent receive the gospel, that means possibly ninety percent of people have reservations about the gospel and yet want to hear more. This is one indicator that it is appropriate for churches to make efforts to reach this majority, who need to hear more about the gospel. The responses to the gospel in Athens support the notion that there is a place for Christians to give seekers a proper understanding of the gospel before expecting them to make an informed commitment to Jesus Christ. Most of our evangelistic strategies today are aimed at the five percent who will eventually believe, but very few of our outreach energies are targeted toward the ninety percent who naturally want to hear more before making any serious commitment to Christ. There is a need for a pre-discipleship process in our strategies in evangelism today.

A MISSING ELEMENT IN EVANGELISM

Given that the church's attempts to make disciples are frequently ineffective, the church has many reasons to pause and rethink how it can improve its evangelistic efforts. We need to give serious consideration to the process of pre-discipleship in future attempts of evangelism. One area in which the church needs to bring change is in the negative understanding that society often has of evangelism. Brian McLaren points out that "on the street, evangelism is equated with pressure. It means selling God as if God were vinyl siding, replacement windows, or a mortgage refinancing service. It means shoving your ideas down someone's throat, threatening him with hell if he does not capitulate to your logic or Scripture-quoting."[33] McLaren suggests that instead of defining evangelism as a battle or crusade to be engaged in the modern world, it should be seen as a dance in the postmodern

---

[33] Brian D. McLaren, *More Ready Than You Realize,* (Grand Rapids, MI: Zondervan, 2002), 12.

matrix. McLaren understands Jesus' style of evangelism as "evangelism that flows like a dance."[34]

The church needs to better motivate Christians to be consistent soul-winners. Bailey Smith says that motivating Christians "is not an easy task. It is estimated, for instance, that only five out of one hundred Christians ever win just one person to Christ in a lifetime."[35] Perhaps the reason why many Christians are not motivated to evangelize is that many do not embrace the modern image of the personal evangelist. Some Christians have an image of the personal evangelist as an aggressive salesperson with an evangelistic sales pitch that manipulates unsuspecting people toward closing a deal with the Lord. If evangelism is reduced to one methodology, then those who feel uneasy with it will neither practice it nor embrace it. One's passion for souls should not be lost in the distaste for a certain methodology. Evangelism must make sense in the context of Christian life.

There is also the value of adopting relational methods of evangelism. According to studies done by Win and Charles Arn, between seventy-five and ninety percent of those who become disciples of Christ come through a friend or a relative. The Arns suggest that the οικος, Greek for "household," refers not only to family, but also servants, servant's family, friends, and even business associates. They propose that οικος is those in one's sphere of influence who are the most likely group to be evangelized. They conclude that "webs of common kinship (the larger family), common friendship (friends and neighbors) and common associates (special interests, work relationships, and recreation) are still the paths most people follow in becoming Christians today."[36]

If Win and Charles Arn's studies are accurate, it would make sense for those doing evangelism to move away from the confrontational styles of evangelism and more towards a relational process. The need is to first connect with people and then, in time, ground them in Christian teaching on the kingdom of God. This is another indicator of the need

---

[34] Ibid., 15.
[35] Bailey E. Smith, *Real Evangelism* (Nashville: Word Publishing, 1999), 166.
[36] Win Arn and Charles Arn, *The Master's Plan for Making Disciples* (Pasadena, CA: Church Growth Press, 1982), 43.

for a pre-discipleship process in evangelism. Some thinkers go so far as to suggest that the church needs to start using a catechetical approach again. William J. Abraham writes,

> Proclamation must be intimately linked to the grounding of people in the kingdom of God. We shall see shortly that proclamation will in fact be carried over into the actual process of initiation, but this requires that we specify more carefully what we have in mind regarding the concrete particulars of initiation. In essence, what I am suggesting is that the church needs to reinstate the institution of the catechumenate.[37]

The catechumenate has a long history. As Robert Webber points out, it was the practice of the early church.

> From the very beginning of the faith, baptism was the primary symbol of coming into the church. By the fourth century the process of baptism was two or three years in length and was marked by four distinct periods of growth and three stages or passage rites. The first stage was that of inquiry (seeker stage); the second was that of the catechumenate (hearer stage); the third was the period of purification and enlightenment (kneeler stage); and the fourth was entrance into the full life of the church (faithful stage). Each stage of development concluded with a passage right that carried the person into the next stage. These passage rites are the rite of welcome, the rite of election, the rite of initiation (baptism).[38]

---

[37] William J. Abraham, *The Logic of Evangelism* (Grand Rapids, Michigan: Wm B. Eerdmans Publishing, 1989, reprint 1996), 174.
[38] Robert E. Webber, *Ancient-Future Faith: Rethinking Evangelicalism for a Postmodern World* (Grand Rapids, Michigan: Baker Books, 1999), 147.

The North American church also needs to address the problems caused by the lack of common values and ways of seeing life in postmodernism. The postmodern mindset is also a post-Christian mindset. Many approaches to evangelism that worked in a context with people who had some Christian background are no longer as effective. Author Stanley Grenz pointed out that in the common rejection to metanarratives, postmodernists embrace tolerance and the affirmation and celebration of diversity. Grenz writes,

> The celebration of cultural diversity does not merely lead to eclecticism as the "style" of postmodernity; more importantly, it overthrows the whole notion of a common standard by which people can measure, judge, or value ideas, opinions, or even aspects of lifestyle. The result is a "centerless" society, one that lacks any clear focus that unites the diverse and divergent elements within it into a single whole. As the center dissolves, the former mass society devolves into a conglomerate of societies, which may have little in common apart from geographic proximity.[39]

Grenz concludes that in order for evangelicals to make an impact in postmodernity, "the way forward is for evangelicals to take the lead in renewing a theological 'center' that can meet the challenges of the postmodern, and in some sense post-theological, situation in which the church now finds itself."[40] He points out that to have a renewed center, evangelicals must be focused on the gospel. He writes,

> A renewed center that is truly evangelical must be characterized above all by a focus on the gospel. As has been noted repeatedly in the previous chapters, to

---

[39] Stanley J. Grenz, *Renewing The Center: Evangelical Thinking in a Post-Theological Era* (Grand Rapids, Michigan: Baker Academic, 2000), 174.
[40] Ibid., 331.

be "evangelical" means to be centered on the gospel. Consequently, evangelicals are a gospel people. They are a people committed to hearing, living out, and sharing the good news of God's saving action that brings forgiveness, transforms life, and creates a new community. As gospel people, evangelicals continually set forth the truth that the center of the church is the gospel and that the church, therefore, must be gospel-centered.[41]

Now the church must begin to find a way for postmodernists to gain a foundation for the gospel to flourish. The catechumenate may provide a process in which postmodernists can begin to embrace truths about Jesus before making a commitment to the Lord.

In rethinking evangelism, one must consider the pre-discipleship process. This process must be a part of the work of the evangelist. MacArthur writes, "The primary duty in evangelism, then, must be to demonstrate the truth of Christianity from the Scriptures."[42] Pre-discipleship does just that. It helps searchers go through an intensive study of the word of God, examining the law of God. It allows for a careful examination, which reveals the truth of God and the will of God. It is important that the evangelistic efforts of the present day church expose seekers to the word of God. In the end, though, whatever method is used, one must evangelize in harmony with the Holy Spirit. Bill Hybels writes, "These days, I'm more convinced than ever that the absolute *highest* value in personal evangelism is staying attuned to and cooperative with the Holy Spirit."[43] Evangelism today must be fluid, patient, and sensitive to the Spirit of God. Central to it is a process of where the seeker studies the word of God in pre-discipleship.

---

[41] Ibid., 337.
[42] MacArthur, *Acts 13–28,* 121–122.
[43] Bill Hybels, *Just Walk Across the Room* (Grand Rapids, MI: Zondervan, 2006), 35.

CHAPTER THREE:

THE BIBLICAL PRACTICE OF PRE-DISCIPLESHIP

If pre-discipleship is a forgotten and key component of evangelism, where do we find it in the Scriptures? Any seemingly new approach to evangelism must not be created out of thin air, or else it will be another manmade idea destined to fail at producing disciples. Instead, all our approaches to evangelism must at least have a biblical and theological basis in order for them to find any success in building disciples. It is important to understand that nearly every believer in the New Testament came to Christ through a pre-discipleship process, a process that involved a personal search for God through the examination of Scripture.

PRE-DISCIPLESHIP IN NEW TESTAMENT CONVERSIONS

The validity of the pre-discipleship process as a means of evangelism is demonstrated in the pages of the New Testament. The pre-discipleship process was more the norm than the exception among New Testament Christians. Before they made commitments to become followers of Christ, the converts to Christianity, first the Jews and then the Gentiles, were introduced to Christianity through pre-discipleship. When Jesus approached the disciples and said, "Follow me,"[44] they were prepared to make a commitment to become a disciple of Jesus because they were grounded in the Scriptures before they met Jesus. The Gentiles who came to Christ also had a foundation in the Scriptures.

---

[44] Mark 2:14 NIV.

Pre-Discipleship among the Jews

The first converts to Christianity in the New Testament were Jews and, as this section will show, nearly every convert to Christianity from Judaism had a foundational understanding of the Scriptures. Their knowledge explains the reactions and responses of many of the disciples, and of Paul, to their encounters with Jesus.

Tradition of pre-discipleship. The study of pre-discipleship among the Jews begins with understanding the historical context of discipleship among the Jews. The practice of discipleship, which existed before the days of Jesus, was often associated with prophets and rabbis. The prophet Isaiah first used the word disciple: *"Bind up the testimony and seal up the law among my disciples"* (Isaiah 8:16). The Old Testament has several examples of mentor-protégé or master-disciple relationships, as in the cases of Moses and Joshua, Elijah and Elisha, and Jeremiah and Baruch. "The disciple's education was acquired through his ministering to the needs of the prophet. This type of training resembled the rabbinic concept of *shimmush,* attendance upon a master."[45]

The Mishnah, which described a Jewish man's stages of life, reveals that study was a significant aspect of the Jewish way of life and that education was associated with the study of Scripture. The Mishnah said that

> At five years old [one is fit] for the Scripture, at ten years for the Mishnah, at thirteen for [the fulfilling of] the commandments, at fifteen for the Talmud, at eighteen for the bride-chamber, at twenty for pursuing [a calling], at thirty for authority, at forty for discernment, at fifty for counsel, at sixty for to be an elder, at seventy for grey hairs, at eighty for special strength, at ninety for bowed back, and at a hundred a

---

[45] Encyclopaedia Judaica, 1st printing, s. v. "education," *In the Biblical Period,* by Aaron Demsky Moriel (Jerusalem: Keter Publishing House Ltd., 1971), 396.

man is as one that has [already] died and passed away and ceased from the world.[46]

Jewish boys as young as five began their education in a system with three levels of learning. The first level was called *Bet Sefer*, house of the book, in which boys from five to ten years of age learned under the instruction of their father at the local synagogue. "In biblical times, the family particularly the father was the source of education. After that time, however, the growing demands of life and the expanding boundaries of Torah study made an institutional framework necessary."[47] At this stage, boys were taught the Torah and to observe the *mitzvahs,* the duties, obligations, and acts of kindness that are practiced in keeping the law. It was not surprising to find most Jewish boys in Jesus' day had memorized Genesis, Exodus, Leviticus, Numbers, and Deuteronomy when they were young. In describing the learning process in the biblical period, Marvin Wilson writes, "the mechanics of learning required the teacher to listen to the student repeat the lesson back to him verbatim. The most important quality for being a good scholar was a trained and retentive memory."[48] The rabbis in Jesus' day used a teaching technique later known as *remez*, which required a student to recite large portions of related Scripture after the rabbi had quoted a portion of it. When Jesus said on the cross, *"Eloi, Eloi, lama sabachthani?"* (Matthew 27:46), the Jews who heard him would have understood his statement in the context of the twenty-second psalm, which many of them would have memorized.

After Bet Sefer, most boys apprenticed with their fathers in the family trade. However, the best students were given the opportunity to pursue the next level of education: *Bet Talmud*, house of learning. In biblical times, the "synagogues in Jerusalem, each ... had a Bible school (Bet Sefer) for the study of the Bible and a Talmud school (Bet

---

[46] Encyclopaedia Judaica, 1st printing, s. v. "education." *In the Talmud,* by Yehuda Moriel (Jerusalem: Keter Publishing House Ltd., 1971), 400–401
[47] Ibid., 401
[48] Marvin R. Wilson, *Our Father Abraham: Jewish Roots of the Christian Faith* (Grand Rapids, MI: Wm. B. Eerdmans Publishing Company, 1989), 303.

Talmud) for the study of the Mishnah."[49] The students studied the Jewish Bible, also known as the Written Torah or the Tanakh.

During this stage of learning, students were also encouraged to study the Talmud, a collection of rabbinic writings concerning Jewish law and tradition. The Talmud contained the Mishnah, a written collection of the "Oral Torah," which were commentaries on the Scriptures, passed down through generations. Today, Talmud study includes the Gemara, additional commentaries, and interpretations of the Mishnah. It was not uncommon for student by the age of fourteen to have memorized the Jewish Bible, known to Christians as the Old Testament.

These boys were also taught to ask questions as a means of communication and learning. Jacob Neusner writes,

> What makes the Talmud engaging is its mode of representing the Torah: through sustained analysis and argument. Specifically, doing more than systematizing the law, the Talmud encourages analysis. Its unfolding dialogue and contention invite successive generations to join in the inquiry into system and order. The Talmud shows how to apply reason and to practice logic. Through a constant flood of questions and answers, disputes and debates, the Talmud invites us to participate in its arguments and to make its issues our own. In presenting the Torah the Talmud preserves diverse opinion and encourages argument and analysis in an open-ended conversation. Here we listen for echoes of that conversation, aspiring to join in.[50]

That was why Jesus could sit *"among the teachers, listening to them and asking them questions. Everyone who heard him was amazed*

---

[49] Encyclopaedia Judaica, 3rd printing, s. v. "education."
[50] Jacob Neusner, *The Talmud: What It Is and What It Says* (New York: Rowman & Littlefield Publishers, Inc, 2006), viii.

at his understanding and his answers" (Luke 2:46-47). Jesus saw himself as a disciple ready to learn. Campbell Morgan writes about Jesus as a boy in the temple:

> He sat down as a Disciple. They talked to him, and taught him, and asked him questions. He answered them, and they listened in amazement. Then He did what every disciple had the right to do; asked them questions, questions arising out of the religious training He had received at home; and still they were amazed. The thing that amazed the teachers was that this Boy, simple, artless, the grace of God resting upon him, revealed in the answers He gave and the questions He asked, such clarity of apprehension, and insight of mind. They had never had a Boy like that before.[51]

After completing Bet Talmud, most boys returned home to the family business. But the best scholars went on to continue in what was called *yeshivah,* or rabbinical academy. Today, the yeshivah is often associated with an institution of religious learning, as in a seminary, but this was not the case in biblical times. In Jesus' day, this next level of learning was known as Bet Midrash, meaning house of study, where a student would study under a rabbi. "At the age of twelve or thirteen a boy finished his studies at school. If he was gifted and so inclined he went on to a *Bet Midrash* to sit at the feet of teachers of the Law with other adults who studied Torah in their spare time."[52] Midrash comes from the Hebrew word meaning "exposition," with the idea of searching into or examining the Scriptures. "The Midrash is the oldest Jewish exposition of the Hebrew Scriptures, made during the period of

---

[51] G. Campbell Morgan, *The God Who Cares, (Books in the Master of the Word Series), ed.* Lawrence O. Richards, (Old Tappan, NJ: Fleming H. Revell Company, 1987), 65.
[52] S. Safrai and M. Stern, eds., *The Jewish People in the First Century,* vol. 2 (Philadelphia: Fortress Press, 1976), 953.

about fifteen hundred years after the Exile, largely based upon tradition."[53]

The young men studying under a rabbi as a *talmid* (disciple) would follow and observe every one of the behaviours of his rabbi in order to be like his master. This relationship of observation was considered so critical to intellectual and spiritual development that one student, according to the Talmud, even laid under his master's bed.[54] Historian Ray Vander Laan describes the commitment of some talmidim:

> A few (very few) of the most outstanding *Beth Midrash* students sought permission to study with a famous rabbi often leaving home to travel with him for a lengthy period of time. These students were called *talmidim* (*talmid, s.*) in Hebrew, which is translated *disciple*. There is much more to a *talmid* than what we call student. A student wants to know what the teacher knows for the grade, to complete the class or the degree or even out of respect for the teacher. A *talmid* wants to be like the teacher that is to become what the teacher is. That meant that students were passionately devoted to their rabbi and noted everything he did or said. This meant the *rabbi/talmid* relationship was a very intense and personal system of education. As the rabbi lived and taught his understanding of the Scripture his students (*talmidim*) listened and watched and imitated so as to become like him. Eventually they would become teachers passing on a lifestyle to their *talmidim*.[55]

If a rabbi thought that a young man could follow in his footsteps, he would tell him to take the rabbi's yoke upon himself and become the rabbi's disciple. A rabbi's yoke was the rabbi's rules, understanding,

---

[53] Ibid., 184.
[54] Babylonian Talmud Berakhot 62a.
[55] Ray Vander Lann, *Rabbi and Talmidim,* in www.followtherabbi.com/Brix?pageID= 2753, accessed October 24, 2008.

and interpretation of Scripture. The majority of Jews had a great wealth in their knowledge of the Scriptures, and knew the law of the Lord intimately.

Pre-discipleship among the disciples. Jesus, who wanted his disciples to learn from him, asked his disciples to take on the rabbi's yoke. He said, *"Come to me, all you who are weary and burdened, and I will give you rest. Take my yoke upon you and learn from me, for I am gentle and humble in heart, and you will find rest for your souls. For my yoke is easy and my burden is light"* (Matthew 11:28-30). When a rabbi chooses a disciple, he is actually saying to the disciple that he has what it takes to be like him. When Jesus called the fishermen to follow him, he was assuring them that they had what it took to be like him.

It was highly likely that the disciples Jesus called to follow him had already gone through a process of pre-discipleship. They had grown up with at least Bet Sefer, and some may have participated in the more intensive study of Bet Talmud. They were familiar with the Torah and the teachings of the law and knew who the Sovereign God was, so they were theologically prepared to follow Jesus.

Not only had their studies prepared them intellectually to follow Jesus, but they had also prepared the disciples emotionally, so the disciples were ready to make a sound choice. This was important because truly following Jesus is not easy and in Jesus' day not everyone could do it. Jesus warned some of the cost. In one case, a teacher of the law said to Jesus, *"'Teacher, I will follow you wherever you go.' Jesus replied, 'Foxes have holes and birds of the air have nests, but the Son of Man has no place to lay his head'"* (Matthew 8:19-20). Another disciple told Jesus that he would follow him after he has finished his business in burying his father, but Jesus told him, *"Follow me, and let the dead bury their own dead"* (Matthew 8:22). Jesus said to his disciples, *"If anyone would come after me, he must deny himself and take up his cross daily and follow me"* (Luke 9:23). Norval Geldenhuys sums it up this way:

> The privilege and the seriousness of following Christ
> are of such tremendous magnitude that there is no
> room for excuse, for compromise with the world, or

for half-heartedness. What a challenge and inspiration to know that He who calls us to complete devotion and loyalty, himself followed whole-heartedly the road of self-denial—yea, even to the death of the cross.[56]

Jesus also warned the large crowds that were attracted by his power when *"they saw the miraculous signs he had performed on the sick"* (John 6:2) about the costs of discipleship.

> If anyone comes to me and does not hate his father and mother, his wife and children, his brothers and sisters—yes, even his own life—he cannot be my disciple. And anyone who does not carry his cross and follow me cannot be my disciple.
>
> Suppose one of you wants to build a tower. Will he not first sit down and estimate the cost to see if he has enough money to complete it? For if he lays the foundation and is not able to finish it, everyone who sees it will ridicule him, saying, "This fellow began to build and was not able to finish."
>
> Or suppose a king is about to go to war against another king. Will he not first sit down and consider whether he is able with ten thousand men to oppose the one coming against him with twenty thousand? If he is not able, he will send a delegation while the other is still a long way off and will ask for terms of peace. In the same way, any of you who does not give up everything he has cannot be my disciple. (Luke 14:26-33)

---

[56] Norval Geldenhuys, *Commentary on the Gospel of Luke,* The New International Commentary on the New Testament, ed. F.F. Bruce (Grand Rapids, MI: Wm. B. Eerdmans Publishing Company, reprint 1983) 296–297.

The cost of discipleship puts the onus on Christians to prepare those who do not know Jesus to understand the cost so they can make an informed decision. Before people can truly follow Jesus, they must be ready in their mind, emotions, and will. Pre-discipleship is that process in evangelism that prepares a person to be ready, intellectually, emotionally, and volitionally, to become a disciple of Christ.

Pre-discipleship experience of the Apostle Paul. Paul is a classic example of a person prepared to accept Christ because of his prior knowledge. Although he had a dramatic conversion while on his way to the synagogues in Damascus to persecute or kill those who belonged to "the Way," Paul did not make a sudden decision solely based on the drama of the situation. Because Paul was a Jew who grew up in the Jewish system of education, he was prepared for his encounter with Jesus. Paul went through Bet Sefer, Bet Talmud, and studied under a rabbi. He said, *"Under Gamaliel I was thoroughly trained in the law of our fathers and was just as zealous for God as any of you are today"* (Acts 22:3). According to Thomas Walker, "St. Paul had been a disciple of one of the most renowned of Jewish rabbis."[57] The Apostle Paul had the necessary theological preparation to follow Jesus and to respond positively when Jesus challenged his heart and his will.

Pre-discipleship experiences of Jewish believers. In the New Testament period, all the Jewish converts had had some form of pre-discipleship, because, as discussed, most Jews, if not all, were grounded in the word of God and the law of God. For them, following Jesus was not a sudden emotional decision, but a life commitment that a lifestyle of study had prepared them to make.

Because the concept of being a disciple of a rabbi was so ingrained, Jewish believers continued to think of their relationship with Christian leaders in the same way, a habit of loyalty that led to some divisions in the Corinthian church, which Paul had to address. *"My brothers, some from Chloe's household have informed me that there are quarrels among you. What I mean is this: One of you says, 'I follow Paul'; another, 'I follow Apollos'; another, 'I follow Cephas'; still*

---

[57] Thomas Walker, *Acts Of The Apostles* (Grand Rapids, MI: Kregel Publications, 1965), 505.

another, 'I follow Christ.'" (1 Corinthians 1:11-12). Paul quickly clarified that Christians are following Christ. He exhorted the Corinthians to *"follow my example, as I follow the example of Christ"* (1 Corinthians 11:1).

Paul taught the Philippians the same truth: *"Join with others in following my example, brothers, and take note of those who live according to the pattern we gave you"* (Philippians 3:17). The idea was to follow the example of Paul in following Jesus. Paul saw himself as a model of a disciple who imitated his master so he could come closer to God. He told the Thessalonians, *"We did this, not because we do not have the right to such help, but in order to make ourselves a model for you to follow"* (2 Thessalonians 3:9). He understood that all believers are disciples of Christ and are to imitate their master. The Apostle Peter wrote, *"To this you were called, because Christ suffered for you, leaving you an example, that you should follow in his steps"* (1 Peter 2:21).

Pre-Discipleship among the Gentiles

Accounts of conversions in the book of Acts show that Gentiles who converted to Christ had had some form of preparation for making that decision. Robert Allen Black, who writes about the pre-conversion state of those who were converted in the book of Acts, points out that the two things they had in common were that not all were Christians and that all had some form of personal practice of holiness. Black writes, "Although they are not Christians, the majority of Luke's subjects are prepared by their own conversion by their pre-conversion piety."[58] Not only had the Jewish converts to Christianity had a form of personal piety, but so had the Gentile converts.

God fearers. In the first century, Gentile practitioners of Judaism, who were called proselytes or God fearers, had a desire to learn about their Creator and were willing to go to great lengths to know God. Converts to Judaism had to go through a process of study and

---

[58] Robert Allen Black, *"The Conversion Stories In the Act of the Apostles"* (Ph D diss., Candler School of Theology Emory University, 1986), 59.

participate in ceremonies before becoming a Jew. Sidney B. Hornig, in his analysis of conversions to Judaism in New Testament times, writes, "The acceptance of converts, follow the mode of Jewish law, required a definite procedure. Such action was especially important in that there was a constant stress on the purity of the family."[59]

A good number of Gentile converts to Christianity in Acts were described as "God fearers." Safrai says concerning the God fearers in the first century,

> The "fearers of heaven" were Gentiles drawn to Jewish religion who kept some of the observances of Judaism, mainly the celebration of the Sabbath and the abstention from prohibited food, but did not become full proselytes and did not undergo the rite of circumcision.[60]

The term God-fearers, which had first been used in the New Testament, in Acts 2:5, to describe Jews, was first applied to Gentiles in a description of Cornelius in Acts 10. There, it said that Cornelius *"and all his family were devout and God-fearing; he gave generously to those in need and prayed to God regularly"* (Acts 10:2). The men whom Cornelius sent to Peter described Cornelius as *"a righteous and God-fearing man, who is respected by the Jewish people"* (Acts 10:22), a man who had been exposed to the word of God and the law of God. Charles Baker writes,

> It appears from Peter's words that Cornelius was somewhat familiar with the Old Testament prophets, as well as with the story of Jesus, for he says to Cornelius: "That word, I say, ye know, which was published throughout all Judea, and began from

[59] Sidney B. Hoenig, *Conversion During The Talmudic Period,* in *Conversion To Judaism: A history and Analysis,* ed. David Max Eichhorn (New York: Ktav Publishing House, Inc., 1965), 45.
[60] S. Safrai and M. Stern, *The Jewish People in the First Century,* vol. 2 (Philadephia: Fortress Press, 1976), 1158.

Galilee, after the baptism which John preached; how that God anointed Jesus of Nazareth with the Holy Spirit and with power, who went about doing good, and healing all who were oppressed of the devil; for God was with him."[61]

The respect that that Jews had for Cornelius also indicates that this Roman was familiar with the Scriptures. James Montgomery Boice explains that the term also indicated that Cornelius had not made a full commitment to Judaism; he had not been circumcised.

That Cornelius was a "God-fearer" meant that although he worshiped Jehovah he had nevertheless not become a Jew by circumcision. God-fearers were Gentiles who expressed interest in Judaism and attended worship in the synagogue, had to sit in the back as observers rather than as full participants in the community. In the eyes of Jewish people it was a good thing to be a God-fearer. It meant that they were on the right religious track.[62]

Another scholar, Frederick Bruce explains that many God-fearers were attracted by the monotheism and ethics of Judaism.

It is further important to observe that Cornelius, though a Gentile, was a worshipper of the God of Israel. Such Gentiles are commonly called "God-fearers"; while this is not a technical term, it is a convenient one to use. Many Gentiles of those days while not prepared to become full converts to Judaism (the requirement of circumcision being a special stumbling block for men), were attracted by

[61] Charles F. Baker, *Understanding the Book of Acts* (Grand Rapids, MI: Grace Bible College Publications, 1981), 60.
[62] James Montgomery Boice, *Acts: An Expositional Commentary* (Grand Rapids, MI: Baker Books, 1997), 174.

the simple monotheism of Jewish synagogue worship and by the ethical standards of the Jewish way of life. Some of them attended synagogue and became tolerably conversant with the prayers and scripture lessons, which they heard read in the Greek version; some observed with more or less scrupulosity such distinctive Jewish practices as Sabbath observance and abstention from certain kinds of food (notably pork). Cornelius' attachment to the Jewish religion appeared particularly in his regular prayer to the God of Israel and acts of charity to the people of Israel. One may say, indeed, that he had every qualification, short of circumcision, which could satisfy Jewish requirements.[63]

The next reference to God-fearers in Acts was in the context of Paul's ministry in Pisidian Antioch. Paul spoke to the worshippers in the synagogue after the reading of the Law and the Prophets, addressing them as *"men of Israel and you Gentiles who worship God"* (Acts 13:16). Paul later referred to his audience as *"children of Abraham, and you God-fearing Gentiles"* (Acts 13:26).

In the Jewish synagogue in Thessalonica, Paul reasoned with the worshippers from the Scriptures about Christ; that synagogue had Jews and *"a large number of God-fearing Greeks"* (Acts 17:4). who joined Paul and Silas. There is also a reference to *"God-fearing Greeks"* (Acts 17:17) in Athens, who were part of the worshippers in the local synagogue.

The evidence reveals that a large number of Gentiles who became Christian in the book of Acts had experienced a form of pre-discipleship or training in the word of God as "God fearers" before they encountered Jesus. This affirms the need for a pre-discipleship process in the Christian conversion journey and means that pre-discipleship is

---

[63] Frederick F. Bruce, *The Book of Acts,* rev. ed., The New International Commentary on the New Testament (Grand Rapids, MI: William B. Eerdmans Publishing Company, 1988), 203.

part of the biblical conversion process that must be incorporated into evangelism.

Other Gentiles. Some Gentile converts to Christianity were not directly referred to as "God-fearers," but this does not mean that they were not God-fearing Gentiles. Such was the case of the Ethiopian Eunuch. He was either a God-fearing Gentile or a proselyte to Judaism. Gerd Ludemann suggests that

> Luke has deliberately left the religious status of the eunuch in the air —: Apparently he did not venture to describe him as a proselyte because of what he found in his sources; he could not let him appear as a Gentile, because the Gentile mission really begins in chapter 10"—the tradition not only presupposes the latter but also reports that the Gentile was a eunuch.[64]

We can deduce that the Ethiopian eunuch was a worshipper of God because he was on his way back from worship in Jerusalem and was studying the book of Isaiah when Philip approached him with the gospel. It is clear that this man from Ethiopia had had some kind of pre-conversion understanding before he encountered Jesus.

Another Gentile that did not have the label "God-fearer" in the Scriptures was Sergius Paulus, a Roman governor of Cyprus who was described as *"an intelligent man"* (Acts 13:7). This phrase implies that he had been investigating Judaism and was not ignorant of the Scriptures. John MacArthur writes of him, "As an intelligent Roman, the governor no doubt had a keen interest in new philosophies and religious beliefs. That he had in his entourage a Jewish teacher (albeit a renegade one) showed he had some interest in Judaism."[65] Sergius Paulus certainly had enough respect for the Scriptures to send for Barnabas and Saul because he wanted to hear the word of God, which

---

[64] Gerd Lüdemann, *Early Christianity According to the Traditions In Acts,* trans. John Bowden (Minneapolis: Fortress Press, 1989), 105.

[65] John MacArthur Jr., *Acts 13–28* (Chicago: Moody Press, 1996), 9.

indicates that he had a basic understanding of God, his word, and his law before he faced the Christian gospel.

The Gentile businesswoman Lydia, who was already *"a worshiper of God"* (Acts 16:14) when she met Christ, was in a small group of women who regularly gathered to learn and pray. Edith Deen writes, "It can be assumed that this little prayer group of which Lydia was a member had asked for guidance, and Paul had been sent to them for a great purpose, because they were receptive to the truth."[66] When Lydia was confronted with the gospel, the Lord opened her heart to respond to it. She already a basic foundation of spiritual truth that made her fertile soil for the seeds of the gospel. Gien Karssen writes concerning Lydia, "The seed of the Word fell into her heart as if onto prepared ground, and resulted in a new birth."[67] One can only speculate on the extent to which Lydia understood in her pre-discipleship process, but her being prepared to receive the gospel indicates that this process existed in Lydia.

The Philippian jailer was the first person in the book of Acts who embraced the gospel without it being clear that he had had pre-discipleship preparation, yet he seems to have had some knowledge of the gospel. When the terrified jailer found that his prisoners had not fled after the miraculous opening of the prison doors, he asked, *"Sirs, what must I do to be saved?"* (Acts 16:30) The jailer must have had enough information to ask about salvation.

The responses of Paul and Silas were interesting. First, they centered on believing in the Lord Jesus, that the whole message of the gospel centered on Jesus Christ. The Apostle Paul said, *"For I resolved to know nothing while I was with you except Jesus Christ and him crucified"* (1 Corinthians 2:2). Second, it was addressed not only to the individual, but also to the household. The gospel was intended for a community as well as the individual. Third, *"they spoke the word of the Lord to him and to all the others in his house"* (Acts 16:32). This meant that the gospel presentation to the household of the Philippian

---

[66] Edith Deen, *All of the Women of the Bible* (New York: Harper & Row, Publishers, 1955), 223.

[67] Gien Karssen, *Her Name Is Woman,* (Colorado Springs, CO: NavPress, 1976), 189.

jailer was not given in short sound bites but in the context of a deep discussion. The most probable scenario was that the Philippian jailer lived at the prison or next door to it. This may explain how Paul, Silas, and the jailer were in the jail one minute and in the jailer's house the next minute. Fourth, the word of the Lord that was spoken involved a discussion on baptism. Not every person who is baptized is saved, but every person who was saved in the New Testament was baptized. The only exception was the thief on the cross with Jesus, who did not have an opportunity to be baptized. The Philippian jailer went through a traumatic, life-changing experience with God that cemented his faith and that of his household. He understood in one night what might take a period of time for others in pre-discipleship. Based on this, it is evident that not everyone who comes to Christ must go through pre-discipleship. However, it seems that the majority of the converts to Christianity in the New Testament, both Jews and Gentiles, did.

Pre-discipleship among the Bereans. The Bereans were the model in the New Testament for pre-discipleship. When Paul and Silas arrived in Berea, they went straight to the synagogue to proclaim the good news about Christ. It was said that the Bereans *"received the message with great eagerness and examined the Scriptures every day to see if what Paul said was true"* (Acts 17:11). The synagogue in Berea was comprised of Jews, prominent Greek women, and many Greek men who studied the Bible before making a decision about becoming Christians. Frederick F. Bruce writes that this procedure of examining the Scriptures was "worthy of imitation by all who have some new form of religious teaching pressed upon their acceptance."[68]

The process the Bereans used involved examining the Scriptures, digesting the word, and allowing the Spirit to speak through it. The value of this process is examined in the next chapter. It would seem that among the New Testament converts, most of them underwent a pre-discipleship process. In other words, the majority of the converts to Christ in the Scriptures engaged in a process of searching, examining, and studying the Word of God before becoming a child of God. This pre-discipleship process is missing in the majority of our evangelistic

---

[68] Frederick F. Bruce, *The Book of the Acts*, 327.

efforts and is perhaps the key reason why many attempts at evangelism result in numerous decisions for Christ, but few disciples for Him.

CHAPTER FOUR:

THE THEOLOGICAL SUPPORT FOR PRE-DISCIPLESHIP

I met with a non-believing young man who was dating a Christian girl who told me that he felt the pressure from Christians to commit to Christ. I told him that I understood the pressure he must have been feeling and that I could guess the reasons why he was not yet a Christian. He asked me what I thought the reasons were, and I told him that believing in Jesus for him was like being forced to marry a girl before having a chance to date her. "You have been asked to make one of the most important commitments of your life to Jesus Christ," I said, "but you never even went through a courting experience with Him." The young man's eyes lit up and realized that it was acceptable to take time to seriously discover who Jesus was before committing to Him.

Although pre-discipleship was a common practice in the New Testament, there are other passages of Scripture that support the pre-discipleship process. Many parts of the church today do not have a full understanding of the type of preparation some people need before they can respond positively to Christ, and so they think that people can quickly made decisions based on just a little information. Much of what the church has deemed to be "evangelistic efforts" in the New Testament are only small aspects of evangelism and were more related to the reaping aspects than those of sowing and other preparatory work. Jesus said, *"I sent you to reap what you have not worked for. Others have done the hard work, and you have reaped the benefits of their labor"* (John 4:38). This happened because, in the New Testament, calls to commit oneself to Christ were made in the context of people who already knew the Scriptures, which allowed those preaching the gospel to build on their listeners' awareness of the Creator. Thus, the seemingly quick responses found in the Bible were made as the result of a longer process of evangelism, one that included some adequate form of preparation. Before the harvest had been reaped, a longer process of "sowing" had laid the foundation that allowed people to respond positively to the gospel. Many evangelicals, however, have reduced Christian conversion to a decision to be made as though it was merely some imaginary line to be crossed. Not everyone is comfortable making quick decisions, and evangelicals have failed to find ways to work with people who need time to think and reflect before making decisions.

PRE-DISCIPLESHIP IMAGES IN THE NEW TESTAMENT

A number of images used in Scripture to describe the process of conversion support the rationale for using a pre-discipleship process. Jesus used metaphors and parables that support the concept of the process of conversion being both immediate and gradual. It is immediate in the sense that the turning of direction from sin to God is instantaneous. It is gradual in the sense that conversion is a process that takes time in the move toward transformation.

New Birth

One image that contains the ideas of the immediate and the gradual is the new birth. Jesus said, *"I tell you the truth, no one can see the kingdom of God unless he is born again"* (John 3:3) during his discussion with Nicodemus concerning the spiritual birth. Jesus told Nicodemus, *"I tell you the truth, no one can enter the kingdom of God unless he is born of water and the Spirit"* (John 3:5), indicating that the spiritual birth parallels the natural birth. Leon Morris discusses two of the possible parallels:

> "Water" may be connected with procreation. This conception is quite foreign to us and we find it difficult at first to make sense of it. But Odeberg has

gathered an impressive array of passages from rabbinic, Mandaean, and Hermetic sources to show that terms like "water", "rain", "dew", and "drop" are often used of the male semen. If "water" has this meaning here there are two possibilities. Being born "of water" may point to natural birth, which must then be followed by being born "of the Spirit," *i.e.* spiritual regeneration. Or better, we may take "water" and "Spirit" closely together to give a meaning like "spiritual seed."[69]

Just as a child needs time to develop before it is born, so a person needs time to develop understanding before spiritual birth occurs. James noted, *"He chose to give us birth through the word of truth, that we might be a kind of firstfruits of all he created"* (James 1:18). Edmond Hiebert comments, "In this epistle James emphatically calls for Christian conduct as proof of the reality of our new birth, but he clearly insists that this new life must first be implanted by God. 'By the word of truth' names the divine means used in our regeneration."[70]

The spiritual birth begins when the word is implanted in a person. When this spiritual seed enters a person's spirit, it begins to grow until spiritual birth occurs. Too often, however, there have been high expectations of the new birth occurring at the time of spiritual conception. Yet, the image of the new birth suggests that it would be more appropriate to allow a person time to develop spiritually before inducing the new birth. It also points to the importance of Christians involved in evangelism supporting this development, using a process such as pre-discipleship.

---

[69] Leon Morris, *The Gospel According To John* (Grand Rapids, MI: Wm. B. Eerdmans Publishing, 1971), 216.

[70] D. Edmond Hiebert, *The Epistle Of James: Tests of a Living* Faith (Chicago: Moody Press, 1979), 116.

Preparing the Soil

When Jesus taught the parable of the sower and the seed in Matthew 13, he was saying that people respond to the gospel depending on how ready they are to receive it. To illustrate his point, he used the imagery of how different conditions affect the growth of the seed. Jesus explained that the imagery of seed falling on a path where the birds eat it represents those who heard the message about the kingdom, but had it snatched away by the evil one before they could understand it. The seed that sprouts and then quickly withers after falling on rocky ground represents people who initially receive the word with joy only to have it fade because they lack the roots to survive when trouble or persecution come along. The thorny ground where the seeds fall and grow but are choked up by weeds are those who grow soon after receiving the word, only are quickly choked by the *"worries of this life and the deceitfulness of wealth"* (Matthew 13:22). The fourth kind of ground is the good soil that allows seeds to flourish. Jesus said that those who hear the word and understand it produce much fruit, like the good soil that produces fruit a hundred, or sixty, or thirty times what was sown. Charles Price says this seed fulfills its purpose:

> This man "hears the word and understands it. He pro-
> duces a crop, yielding a hundred, sixty or thirty times
> what was sown." He hears the word like the first
> seed, he gets excited like the second, he too lives in
> the world and is subject to all its temptations like the
> third, but his roots are deep, he survives and reprod-
> uces himself. He is successful. This seed in the world
> accomplishes its purpose.[71]

Although Jesus did not discuss the need to create good soil in his parable of the sower, this can be inferred. Even poor soil can be

---

[71] Charles Price, *Matthew* (Guernsey, C.I.: The Guernsey Press Company, Ltd., 1998, reprint 2000), 157.

improved so that it is receptive to seed and supports its growth. Michael Simpson comments on the importance of preparing the soil.

> Farming in modern times is very different than 2000 years ago, but the principles and impacts of planting will always apply. Seed is planted primarily in the furrowed, nourished, and softened soil—soil that has been prepared—otherwise, you are wasting your seed. Scattered seed will still sometimes sprout and grow—it may even bear fruit. But the harvest is so much more plentiful when the seed is planted in soil that has been prepared.[72]

Just as a farmer or gardener prepares the land by first removing the stones, rocks, weeds, and by amending the soil with nutrients, Christians need to prepare the soil so that the planting of the seed of the gospel will result in a bountiful harvest. Pre-discipleship is the preparation of the land needed for planting to be effective. The process of introducing Jesus to unbelievers through a search in the Scriptures can be time-consuming, but in the end will result in mature crops.

Entering the Narrow Gate

Jesus' teaching that finding the way to life is not easy is another example of biblical support for a pre-discipleship process. In the Sermon on the Mount, Jesus said, *"Enter through the narrow gate. For wide is the gate and broad is the road that leads to destruction, and many enter through it. But small is the gate and narrow the road that leads to life, and only a few find it"* (Matthew 7:13-14). The narrow gate is the entrance that leads to eternal life, in contrast to the wide gate that leads to destruction. Jesus said that "only a few find" the narrow gate, which implies that finding eternal life takes effort. MacArthur writes, "The fact that few are those who find God's way implies that it is to be sought diligently. 'And you will seek me and find me, when

---

[72] Simpson, *Permission Evangelism*, 86.

you search for me with all your heart' (Jer. 29:13). No one has ever stumbled into the kingdom or wandered through the narrow gate by accident."[73]

When evangelicals quote Ephesians 2:8-9, *"For it is by grace you have been saved, through faith—and this not from yourselves, it is the gift of God—not by works, so that no one can boast"* (NIV), they rightly point out that no one can earn their salvation. However, some evangelicals equate salvation by grace with effortless salvation. They believe that because salvation is by grace, they do not have to do anything except passively receive it. While salvation is not by works, that does not mean it is obtained without effort. Jesus said, *"Make every effort to enter through the narrow door, because many, I tell you, will try to enter and will not be able to"* (Luke 13:24). In discussing the meaning of "make every effort" or "strive," commentators Jamieson, Fausset, and Brown said, "The word signifies to 'contend' as for the mastery, to "struggle," expressive of the *difficulty* of being saved, as if one would have to *force his way in*."[74]

Could it be that the effort of entering the narrow gate is in the searching, finding, and emptying of oneself to enter with humility? In any case, the concept of searching supports the need for a process of pre-discipleship, where such a search can occur.

Blind Man at Bethsaida

Jesus was once in Bethsaida when some people brought to him a blind man, begging him to touch the man. Jesus led the blind man by hand out of the village and spat on the man's eyes. He then put his hands on the blind man and asked if he saw anything. The blind man said, *"I see people; they look like trees walking around"* (Mark 8:24). Jesus once more put his hands on the man's eyes and his eyes were open, being able to see everything clearly. Why did Jesus take so long to heal this

---

[73] John MacArthur Jr., *Matthew 1-7* The Macarthur New Testament Commentary (Chicago: Moody Press, 1985), 455.

[74] Robert Jamieson, Andrew Fausset, and David Brown, "The Jamieson, Fausset, and Brown Commentary," in *the Bethany Parallel Commentary on the New Testament* (Minneapolis, MN: Bethany House Publishers, 1983), 430.

blind man? We know that Jesus could have given this blind man at Bethsaida immediate sight, like Bartimaeus in Mark 10. The blind man in John 9 was healed after he washed in the Pool of Siloam.

Although we can only speculate as to the reason why Jesus healed the blind man at Bethsaida in two stages, the story may be an object lesson as to how the spiritually blind can come to see. Blind men are one of the biblical illustrations of spiritual conversion. The blind man in John 9 testified, *"One thing I do know. I was blind but now I see!"* (John 9:25) Bartimaeus may be the image of the sudden conversion, as also seen in the conversion of the Apostle Paul. The blind man at Bethsaida could be the image of the conversion of the disciples of Jesus.

The context of the passage concerning the blind man at Bethsaida relates to Jesus' disappointment in his disciples in their lack of understanding. *"Why are you talking about having no bread? Do you still not see or understand? Are you hearts hardened? Do you have eyes but fail to see, and ears but fail to hear? And don't you remember?"* (Mark 8:17-18) The disciples were like the blind man who saw people who looked like trees walking around. They could see, but they could not see clearly. Jesus kept asking them, *"Do you still not understand?"* (Mark 8:21)

Richard Peace argues that "the conversion of the Twelve is a major theme in the Gospel of Mark and, in fact, the organizing principle by which Mark structures his Gospel."[75] He suggests that the whole gospel of Mark is an account of the process of conversion that takes place among the Twelve. The healing of the blind man at Bethsaida is an illustration of that process. Once again, if conversion is more often a gradual process than immediate change, pre-discipleship can be an active agent in that process towards repentance.

Counting the Cost

Proverbs says, *"It is a trap for a man to dedicate something rashly and only later to consider his vows"* (Proverbs 20:25). This proverb spoke

---

[75] Richard V. Peace, *Conversion in the New Testament: Paul and the Twelve*, 107.

about making any kind of commitment rashly, without much thought. Jesus never asked those who wanted to follow him to become his disciples blindly or thoughtlessly. When he was gaining popularity, Jesus said to the crowd, *"If anyone comes to me and does not hate his father and mother, his wife and children, his brothers and sisters—yes, even his own life—he cannot be my disciple. And anyone who does not carry his cross and follow me cannot be my disciple"* (Luke 14:26-27).

Using a couple of stories to illustrate his point, Jesus cautioned the people that following in his steps was not to be done rashly. The first illustration was about a builder who needed to count his cost.

> Suppose one of you wants to build a tower. Will he not first sit down and estimate the cost to see if he has enough money to complete it? For if he lays the foundation and is not able to finish it, everyone who sees it will ridicule him, saying, 'This fellow began to build and was not able to finish.' (Luke 14:28-30)

Becoming a disciple of Jesus was not a commitment to approach lightly. Rather, like the builder, people must count the cost before proceeding. William F. Arndt discusses why:

> Does one really have to carry on analogous investig-ations before joining Christ and his kingdom? Entrance into the blessed realm is free; forgiveness of sin and a place in heaven are there ready to be taken. Why, then, these examinations? What justification is there for urging prospective disciples to count the cost? The answer is obvious. Salvation indeed is free, but to be a disciple of Jesus means that one is engaged in a constant struggle with the forces of evil both about us and in us. To be a follower of our Lord signifies not only that one trusts him for whatever blessings we need, but that one is a lover of good and a foe of everything that is wrong. Regeneration is followed by sanctification, which involves traveling

the steep, narrow path of denial of self. Christianity is the easiest religion in the world and at the same time the most difficult one. Those that hold that Jesus' teaching grants license for serving one's carnal desires are hear shown to be woefully wrong.[76]

The second story Jesus told the crowd was about a king at war.

Or suppose a king is about to go to war against another king. Will he not first sit down and consider whether he is able with ten thousand men to oppose the one coming against him with twenty thousand. If he is not able, he will send a delegation while the other is still a long way off and will ask for terms of peace. In the same way, any of you who does not give up everything he has cannot be my disciple. (Luke 14:31-33)

Again, Jesus was pointing out that one must consider the consequences before becoming his disciple. Alois Stöger writes, "The man who undertakes anything big must first check carefully, to see whether the strength and the means he has are sufficient. The message of the double parable is: think first, then act."[77] Pre-discipleship provides a process in which people can evaluate what it means to follow Jesus so they can make an informed commitment.

This examination of the images and metaphors used for conversion has shown that biblical support exists for pre-discipleship. The image of the new birth shows that the spiritual birth takes time after spiritual conception, which supports the use of pre-discipleship before conversion as a developmental process. The image of preparing the soil is a sensible picture of the need for pre-discipleship. The image of the narrow gate reveals the need for a seeker to search for the way of life, a

---

[76] William F. Arndt, *Luke* (St. Louis: Concordia Publishing House, 1956; reprint in Concordia Classic Commentary Series, 1986), 345.

[77] Alois Stöger, *The Gospel According To St. Luke Volume 2*, ed. John L. McKenzie (New York: Herder and Herder, 1969), 33–34.

search that pre-discipleship can support well. The image of counting the cost reflects the need of potential disciples of Jesus to evaluate their spiritual situation thorough a form of pre-discipleship before making a commitment to Christ. In the next section, pre-discipleship will be examined in how it relates and leads to baptism.

PRE-DISCIPLESHIP AND BAPTISM

Baptism in the New Testament church was a public proclamation of a believer's faith and commonly occurred immediately after a person had made a profession of faith. No intervening period of instruction in the faith was required to prepare a new Christian for baptism. This section examines the immediacy of baptism after a person believed in Christ and the place of pre-discipleship in this practice. In the Great Commission, Jesus instructed his followers again to *"make disciples of all nations, baptizing them in the name of the Father and of the Son and of the Holy Spirit"* (Matthew 28:19). In the New Testament, everyone who professed to follow the Lord was baptized in the name of Jesus, the only exception being the thief on the cross. The majority of followers were baptized immediately, although the Apostle Paul waited three days to be baptized after his conversion. Henry Morris comments on immediacy of baptism:

> When you understand the importance that is conn-
> ected with obedience to baptism, it is easy to
> recognize that there would be ample reason to
> question whether one who refused baptism really had
> saving faith. Every record of a salvation experience
> in connection with the evangelistic ministry of the
> church shows that the convert was baptized immed-
> iately after his salvation.[78]

---

[78] Henry M. Morris III, *Baptism: How Important Is It?* (Denver, CO: Accent Books, 1978), 103–104.

While the immediacy of the baptism was natural in the New Testament, today it is often a delayed process. Though many gospel presentations prepare a person to pray to accept Christ, they do not prepare that person for baptism. The need for subsequent follow-up, such as baptismal classes, indicates that current gospel presentations are weak in preparing people to understand the Christian faith. Pre-discipleship, a practice that leads to authentic discipleship, has been overlooked both in theology and in our practice of it.

The language in the command to "make disciples" in Matthew 28:19-20 is another important clue to the role of pre-discipleship in preparing people for baptism. This command is modified by the participles "baptizing" and "teaching," which clarify what it means to make disciples. G. R. Beasley-Murray explains that there is a strong link to baptism and teaching in disciple-making:

> From the linguistic point of view, Lindblom has pointed out that when participles in Greek are co-ordinated with the main verb they are linked by means of a καί, or τε... καί, or δέ: if they follow one another without any such binding conjunction or particle they must be viewed as depending on one another or depending in differing ways on the chief verb. This accords with the situation envisaged in the Commission, that proclamation of the redemption of Christ should be made and those responding in repentance and faith should be baptized and come under instruction.[79]

Beasley-Murray concluded that "baptizing belongs to the means by which a disciple is made. The instruction comes after."[80] Like many, Beasley-Murray assumed that the instruction comes after baptism and not before it. Yet, as he pointed out, the language of the text in the

[79] G.R. Beasley-Murray, *Baptism In The New Testament* (Grand Rapids, MI: Wm B. Eerdmans Publishing, 1962), 89.
[80] Ibid.

Great Commission allows for the teaching to occur before baptism. Pre-discipleship can bring those who will believe to the place where they have enough understanding to enter the waters of baptism.

Other Scriptures seem to imply that people receive teaching before baptism. The writer of Hebrews chastised the Jewish believers concerning their immature faith and encouraged them to move on from the elementary truths of God's word into more solid food.

> We have much to say about this, but it is hard to explain because you are slow to learn. In fact, though by this time you ought to be teachers, you need someone to teach you the elementary truths of God's word all over again. You need milk, not solid food! Anyone who lives on milk, being still an infant, is not acquainted with the teaching about righteousness. But solid food is for the mature, who by constant use have trained themselves to distinguish good from evil. Therefore, let us leave the elementary teachings about Christ and go on to maturity, not laying again the foundation of repentance from acts that lead to death, and of faith in God, instruction about baptisms, the laying on of hands, the resurrection of the dead, and eternal judgment. (Hebrews 5:11-6:2)

Part of this elementary teaching was instruction about baptism, though whether the pre-baptismal teaching included part or all of the elementary truths mentioned in Hebrews is unknown. Jamieson, Fausset, and Brown describe the elementary teachings mentioned as a catechism: "the six particulars here specified had been, as it were, *the Christian Catechism* of the Old Testament."[81]

The early post-apostolic church practiced a process of catechesis so that new converts were taught before baptism. Robert Bradley writes concerning the church near the end of the second century, "For catechesis, the elementary systematic teaching of the faith, though

---

[81] Jamieson, Fausset, and Brown, 1297.

clearly distinct from evangelization (and apologetics) on the one hand, and from homiletics (and theology) on the other, nevertheless is closely related to them in the living milieu of the historical church."[82] Bradley described the catechumenate as part of the process before baptism.

> The catechumenate—whatever might be its overall duration—always ended within a definite time-frame: the season of Lent. This tie-in was detailed and elaborate, clearly conveying the supreme importance attached to the annual celebration of the Paschal Mystery as the time par excellence for the renewal of the Church in her members ... This ceremony usually took place on Palm Sunday, and so symbolized the completion, by the official teacher of the faith, of the catechumen's formal instruction. And thus they were ready for their formal profession of faith at the Easter Vigil, and their reception of the sacraments of baptism, confirmation and Holy Eucharist.[83]

It is evident that the pre-discipleship process was practiced in the New Testament and in the early church before baptism. The catechumenate gave evidence that converts to Christianity had systematic teaching before they could be baptized. This was another confirmation of the existence of a pre-discipleship process in the early church.

PRE-DISCIPLESHIP AND THEOLOGICAL PERSUASIONS

This section considers how pre-discipleship may be understood by theologians to be a process in the spectrums of both Calvinistic and Arminian theological persuasions. It is necessary to understand that pre-discipleship is not the practice of one theological persuasion, but one that resonates with many theological persuasions. Calvinists may

---

[82] Robert I. Bradley, *The Roman Catechism in the Catechetical Tradition of the Church* (Lanham, MD: University Press of America,1990), 9.
[83] Ibid., 14.

see pre-discipleship as God's sovereign means of drawing the elect toward his irresistible grace. According to John Calvin, "faith is the knowledge of the divine will towards us, discovered from his Word."[84] Pre-discipleship, to the Calvinist, would be the act of faith by the elect seeking God through his word. Calvin wrote,

> We do not deny that it is the nature of faith to assent to God's truth in whatever way he speaks: we only want to find out what faith can find in God's Word, to lean and to rely upon. When conscience is only aware of wrath and indignation, how can it do anything but tremble and be afraid and how can it avoid turning away from the God whom it dreads? But faith ought to seek God, not turn from him.[85]

Arminians may see pre-discipleship as man's initial response to God's grace. Those in the Arminian camp view seekers of God to be people who have God's grace working in their lives. Corrie Cieslukowski and Elmer Colyer said, "The Methodist Societies (roughly analogous to a congregation) and the small-group class meetings were open to anyone who was seeking God, because if you were a seeker it could only mean that God's convicting grace was already at work in your life."[86]

Theological pre-discipleship has a legitimate place in both Calvinist and Arminian views of *Ordo Salutis* ("the order of salvation"). Pre-discipleship would resonate with the Reformed view because it would be one of the steps or stages in the salvation of a believer in relation to election, foreknowledge, predestination, redemption, regeneration, justification, sanctification, and glorification. Historically, the Reformed position believed that the regeneration of the spirit in man was a prerequisite to faith and repentance. Pre-

---

[84] John Calvin, *The Institutes of Christian Religion,* edited by Tony Lane and Hilary Osborne (Grand Rapids, MI: Baker Book House, 1987), 145.
[85] Ibid, 145–146.
[86] Corrie M. Aukema Cieslukowski and Elmer M. Colyer, "Wesley's Trinitarian Ordo Salutis," *Reformation and Revival* 14 (Number 4, 2005): 105–131.

discipleship would be a means the Spirit of God uses to bring clarity regarding the seeker's need for salvation in the process of regeneration.

On the other hand, the Arminian position on *Ordo Salutis* is that election is based on one's faith and response to the gospel. Arminians may understand pre-discipleship as the beginning of man's response toward the grace of God. The fourth article of Arminianism stated:

> That man has not saving grace of himself, nor of the energy of his free-will, inasmuch as he, in the state of apostasy and sin, can of and by himself neither think, will, nor do anything that is truly good (such as saving faith eminently is); but that it is needful that he be born again of God in Christ, through his Holy Spirit, and renewed in understanding, inclination, or will, and all his powers, in order that he may rightly understand, think, will, and effect what is truly good, according to the word of Christ.[87]

Thus, pre-discipleship would be seen as the initial positive response to God's grace rather than a rejection of God's grace. It would be part of the process of faith before regeneration. Gordon Olson writes, "Man is unable to contribute one iota to his own salvation, but we are held accountable for our response to God's revelation, both general and special, in the gospel. Just as Lucifer and Adam were held responsible for the exercise of their free wills in sin against God, just as really, all humans, although enslaved to sin are accountable to exercise their wills in repentance and faith. Indeed, we are even commanded to seek God."[88]

The process of pre-discipleship is not an obscure teaching in a corner of theological thought but instead fits into both spectrums of Calvinistic and Arminian persuasions. Pre-discipleship is a practice that

---

[87] David Nettleton, *Chosen to Salvation: Select Thought on the Doctrine of Election* (Schaumburg, IL: Regular Baptist Press, 1983), 41.
[88] C. Gordon Olson, *Beyond Calvinism and Arminianism: An Inductive, Mediate Theology of Salvation* (Cedar Knolls, NJ: Global Gospel Publishers, 2002), 110.

is biblically based and theologically sound. It is a practice that needs to be highlighted again in our evangelism.

CHAPTER FIVE:

PRE-DISCIPLESHIP IN EVANGELISM

The ineffectiveness of making disciples in many evangelistic efforts demands an examination of the approaches being used to share the gospel with the world. Only after an evaluation of the various kinds of evangelism practiced today can one come away with new insights on how Christians can most effectively reach the world for Christ. Because so much has been written on evangelism, with such diverse views of what it involves, it is important to begin by defining evangelism and the work of the evangelist in order to lay the foundation for the rest of the discussion on the topic. The examination of the various types of outreach done in encounter and process evangelism will lead to a consideration of an alternative concept for reaching the lost for Christ.

DEFINITIONS OF EVANGELISM

The definitions of evangelism in the Christian community often do not include discipleship, which creates problems for the church because the biblical understanding of evangelism includes discipleship. This chapter attempts to provide a definition, first by looking at existing views of evangelism and then by describing the biblical understanding of evangelism and the work of the evangelist. The church today has had difficulty developing a holistic definition of evangelism. Ben Campbell Johnson points out the shortcomings in the understanding of evangelism in the local church. He writes, "Evangelism is being defined popularly as "everything we do." Consequently, the basic task of reaching new persons for Christ, incorporating them into the church, and equipping them for ministry is being gravely neglected."[89] Darius Salter notes the plurality of definitions for evangelism:

> There are scores of synonyms for evangelism throughout the history of the English language, most of which are included in the New Testament. They include argue, speak, talk, witness, and most common, tell. In all, 41 synonyms are used an amazing 2,468 times in the New Testament.[90]

Salter later attempts to form a working definition of evangelism that embraced discipleship and concludes,

> I assume that when Paul told Timothy to do the work of an "evangelist," there was a mutually understood job description, though it may not have been rigidly spelled out. Indeed, if a person is to remain a new creature in Christ Jesus, he or she will have to be a part of the community of God and its enterprises. Some enterprises will be much more evangelistically oriented than others; it will not always be easy to define which are and which are not. In H.W. Gensichen's words, "Everything the Church is and does must have a missionary *dimension*, but not everything has a missionary *intention*." It is of primary importance that we address intentional evangelism, while not truncating the evangelistic enterprise from the total gamut of discipleship.[91]

In 1918, the Archbishop's Committee on Evangelism in England collectively attempted to define evangelism. The committee concluded

---

[89] Ben Campbell Johnson, *Rethinking Evangelism: A Theological Approach* (Philadelphia: Westminster Press, 1987), 11–12.
[90] Darius Salter, *American Evangelism: Its Theology and Practice* (Grand Rapids, MI: Baker Books, 1996), 21.
[91] Ibid., 29.

that "to evangelize is so to present Christ Jesus in the power of the Holy Spirit, that men shall come to put their trust in God through him, to accept him as their Savior and serve him as their King in the fellowship of His Church."[92] In this definition, the concept of discipleship was implied but not mentioned.

In 1966, evangelical leaders at the Berlin World Congress on Evangelism developed a working definition of evangelism:

> Evangelism is the proclamation of the Gospel of the crucified and risen Christ, the only Redeemer of men, according to the Scriptures, with the purpose of persuading condemned and lost sinners to put their trust in God by receiving and accepting Christ as Savior through the power of the Holy Spirit, and to serve Christ as Lord in every calling of life and in the fellowship of His Church, looking toward the day of His coming in glory.[93]

Again this definition did not highlight the disciple-making component of evangelism.

Another global conference on evangelism, Amsterdam 2000, which reportedly drew the largest number of Christian leaders ever assembled, from the widest national, ethnic, linguistic, cultural and denominational backgrounds, did include a discipleship component in the Amsterdam Declaration:

> Derived from the Greek word *euangelizesthai*, "to tell glad tidings," this word signifies making known the Gospel of Jesus Christ so that people may trust in God through him, receiving him as their Savior and serving him as their Lord in the fellowship of His Church. Evangelism involves declaring what God has

---

[92] Carl F.H. Henry, *Evangelicals at the Brink of Crisis: Significance of the World Congress on Evangelism* (Waco, TX: Word Books, 1967), 37.
[93] Ibid.

done for our salvation and calling on the hearers to become disciples of Jesus through repentance from sin and personal faith in him.[94]

With the inclusion of making disciples in the definition of evangelism, evangelicals began to understand the fuller meaning of evangelism. What then is the biblical meaning of evangelism? The verb εὐαγγελίζω, meaning "to proclaim as good tidings, to evangelize, to bring, to announce, to preach good news" is found fifty-four times in the New Testament. The noun εὐαγγέλιον, translated as "gospel" or "good news," is found seventy-six times in the New Testament.

Εὐαγγελίστής, meaning "evangelist," which is found three times in the New Testament, has a different meaning than the one understood by many Evangelicals today. Each time the "evangelist" is mentioned, it means someone who shared the gospel rather than a person who held a position in a church. According to Gerhard Kittel, "εὐαγγελίστής originally denotes a function rather than an office, and there can have been little difference between an apostle and an evangelist, all apostles being evangelists."[95] An evangelist was someone who shared the good news rather than a person with a specific title in the church. The first time εὐαγγελίστής is mentioned in the Scriptures is in Acts 21:8, where Luke called a man named Philip "the evangelist" to distinguish him from Philip the apostle. Philip the evangelist was the same Philip who was one of the seven chosen in Jerusalem to wait on tables (Acts 6:5) and who led the Ethiopian eunuch to Jesus. The writer of Acts used "evangelist" as a function that Philip engaged in rather than a position that he held in the church.

The second passage where εὐαγγελίστής is found is in Ephesians 4, a classic passage.

It was he who gave some to be apostles, some to be prophets, some to be evangelists, and some to be

---

[94] Amsterdam 2000, *The Mission of an Evangelist: Amsterdam 2000* (Minneapolis, MN: World Wide Publications, 2001), 458.
[95] Gerhard Kittel, ed., *Theological Dictionary of the New Testament*, trans. Geoffrey W. Bromiley (Grand Rapids, MI: Wm. B. Eerdmans Publishing Company, 1978), 737.

> pastors and teachers, to prepare God's people for
> works of service, so that the body of Christ may be
> built up until we all reach unity in the faith and in the
> knowledge of the Son of God and become mature,
> attaining to the whole measure of the fullness of
> Christ. (Ephesians 4:11-13)

This makes it clear that the goal of the apostles, prophets, evangelists, pastors, and teachers was to bring the whole body of Christ to maturity, which indicates the goal of making disciples. J. Armitage Robinson pointed out in the *Didaché* that the "apostles" a generation later were like present day "missionaries." They would "seem to correspond to the evangelists of St. Paul's catalogue who carried the Gospel to regions hitherto unevangelized. This mention of them establishes beyond further question of that wider us of the name 'apostle.'"[96] While the early church leaders had different titles, they all had the same purpose—to bring the body of Christ to maturity. If making disciples was the mandate, some of the ministries of the apostles, prophets, evangelists, pastors, and teachers would overlap. E. K. Simpson writes, "The New Testament affords no hint of a priestly caste, 'commanding all the approaches of the soul to him,' usurpers of the title they clutch at; but the universal priesthood of believers, each occupying his proper place in the body of Christ, has its clear authorization. In the theocracy of grace there is in fact no laity."[97] The purpose of every ministry is disciple-making, to bring all to maturity in Christ.

The third passage where εὐαγγελίστής is found is 2 Timothy 4, where Paul encourages Timothy to *"do the work of an evangelist"* (2 Timothy 4:5). This encouragement to evangelize was found in the context of discipleship. However, many, like John Philips, have tried to understand the work of the evangelist through modern eyes instead of those of the first century.

---

[96] J. Armitage Robinson, *Commentary on Ephesians: The Greek Text with Notes and Indexes* (Grand Rapids, MI: Kregel Publications, 1979), 98.
[97] E.K. Simpson and F.F. Bruce, *Commentary on the Epistles to the Ephesians and Colossians* (Grand Rapids, MI: Wm. B. Eerdmans Publishing, 1957, reprint 1982), 95.

The pastor is essentially a shepherd. His task is to feed, protect, and care for the flock entrusted to his care. The evangelist, on the other hand, is essentially a soul winner. When he preaches, people come under conviction and turn to Christ, sometimes in great numbers. Timothy did not have that *gift* of the evangelist; he was to "do the *work* of an evangelist." He was to preach the gospel and extend the invitation; he was to talk to people about Christ; he was to be a witness and seek to lead people to Christ.[98]

The work of the evangelist must first be understood through the eyes of first century readers. However, Philips tries to apply a crusade style of evangelism to the role of the evangelist, ignoring the discipleship aspects of Paul's letter to Timothy. Ronald A. Ward attempts to change the emphasis of the work of an evangelist to mean that evangelism is work. He is pointing out that what the evangelist does is work and more than just talk. Ward writes, "Paul however when exhorting Timothy did not emphasize speech. To preach the gospel is *work*. This should arrest those who cynically say that the minister merely "talks." Just as the deeds of Jesus were words in action (they had a message) and his words had effects of deeds, so the words of the *evangelist* have mighty power and accomplish much. His words are *work*."[99] However, Ward's understanding of the work of the evangelist is also devoid of the aspect of making disciples.

A significant aspect of the work of the evangelist is making disciples. The work of the evangelist in the Bible is described in the context of making disciples. The Great Commission describes the work of the evangelist as teaching the gospel to the lost nations so that they will become disciples of Christ. The context of the Ephesians passage

---

[98] John Phillips, *Exploring The Pastoral Epistles: An Expository Commentary* The John Phillips Commentary Series (Grand Rapids, MI: Kregel Publications, 2004), 436–437.
[99] Ronald A. Ward, *Commentary on 1 and 2 Timothy and Titus* (Waco, TX: Word Books, Publisher, 1974), 209.

implies that the work of the evangelist was to bring the lost into maturity in Christ. The context of the 2 Timothy letter is discipleship. Paul wrote, *"And the things you have heard me say in the presence of many witnesses entrust to reliable men who will also be qualified to teach others"* (2 Timothy 2:2). In commenting about the work of an evangelist, N. A. Woychuk writes, "More accurately and especially as it would apply to every believer, it would read, 'Let your work be evangelistic in nature.' 'Be a carrier of the good tidings.'"[100]

If the role of a pastor is to bring a person from where he is spiritually to maturity in Christ, then Paul's encouragement to Timothy to do the work of an evangelist is to continue to make disciples with an evangelistic component in the process. If the New Testament under-standing of the work of an evangelist was to bring the unsaved to maturity in Christ, this means the work of the evangelist involved an element of teaching and discipleship. The first century Christians understood work of the evangelist as being one of bringing people to Jesus through a process of making disciples. This practice of making disciples with believers and unbelievers allows the concept of pre-discipleship to fit in perfectly with the description of the work of the evangelist.

EVALUATIONS OF TYPES OF EVANGELISM

Today Christians use many methods in their attempt to reach the world for Christ, and evangelistic efforts can range from a long-term relationship with a friend to a short encounter with a stranger. It could involve a quiet meal over dinner to a massive crusade involving thousands of people. Because of this, it is important to identify the various types of evangelistic efforts in the church today, in order to recognize the diverse ways in which people come to faith in Christ. Richard Peace provides a useful framework for identifying the various types of evangelistic efforts. He identifies two types of evangelism in use today, encounter evangelism and process evangelism. Encounter

---

[100] N.A. Woychuk, *an Exposition of Second Timothy: Inspirational and Practical* (Old Tappan, NJ: Fleming H. Revell Company, 1973), 142.

evangelism involves using event-oriented methods of outreach, in contrast to process evangelism, which tends to be relational in nature.

Encounter Evangelism

The first type of evangelism, as framed by Richard V. Peace, is encounter evangelism. It is based on the assumption that most conversions occur dramatically, like that of the Apostle Paul. Encounter evangelism attempts to bring people to meet with Jesus Christ. Peace defines encounter evangelism:

> This is the term I use for those methods of outreach which seek to bring about in the lives of people Pauline-like encounters with Jesus. In large part, these are the evangelistic methodologies that have been used by the church since World War II. The result is that when you use the word "evangelism," what comes to mind for most people is activities of this sort. The question is: Have we got it right? When we examine these ways of outreach on the basis of the two paradigms for conversion in the New Testament, what do we find?[101]

Peace identifies three types of outreach that could be called encounter evangelism: mass evangelism, personal evangelism, and media evangelism.

Often evangelism has been associated with the mass crusades and a well-known evangelist. On the surface, this method seems to be an effective way of preaching the gospel. However, the results raise questions about its effectiveness. The problem with mass evangelism, as mentioned in chapter one, is that while statistics may suggest a large number people have made decisions for Christ, in reality disciples of

---

[101] Richard V. Peace, *Conversion in the New Testament: Paul and the Twelve* (Grand Rapids, MI: Wm B. Eerdmans Publishing Company, 1999), 287.

Christ are not being produced. Jerry Reed, who headed the follow-up for an Evangelism-in-Depth crusade in Quito, Ecuador, reports,

> By the close of the crusade 1,234 people had responded to the evangelist's invitation to commit their lives to Jesus Christ. We had well-trained counselors and a good follow-up system net-working with most of the area churches and leaders. Yet one year later when I went back to study the results of that big evangelistic campaign, only 64 people (5 percent) could be found in churches and most of those churches were within easy walking distance of the coliseum where the meetings had been held … I might add that the net results for Ecuador of that year-long saturation-evangelism thrust of Evangel-ism-in-Depth, was a grand total of sixteen more people added to the church than would have been added without the movement![102]

Reed then observes that "the same was true for the Luis Palau crusade a couple of years later."[103] It seems that many mass evangelistic efforts have left the body of Christ with only a few church goers and likely even fewer disciples.

Personal evangelism differs from mass evangelism in that the focus is on the individual as opposed to the group. The presentation is made through a personal testimony with the presenter, using an outline of a plan of salvation. In personal evangelism, the challenge to make a commitment to Christ is presented in a form of dialogue rather than as an invitation following a sermon.

One form of personal evangelism is visitation, a method in use as early as the 1870s, when Dwight L. Moody employed it in his crusades. Throughout the twentieth century, it has been developed and refined in

---

[102] Jerry Reed, "Lasting Fruit in Evangelism" in *Journal of the Academy for Evangelism in Theological Education* 11 (1995–96), 48–49.
[103] Ibid., 49.

North American churches. In the 1970s, personal evangelism gained popularity among Christian churches and many programs were developed. The popular Evangelism Explosion, developed by James Kennedy, pastor of the Coral Ridge Presbyterian Church in Fort Lauderdale, Florida, trained Christians to direct their conversations with people towards a prepared presentation of the gospel. Personal evangelism then became a sales pitch in which the gospel was a product and the work of the evangelist was to close the deal. While the visitation method has brought many into the kingdom and mobilized Christians in many churches to engage in active evangelism, it is not without its drawbacks. One problem is that people who might be converted through this type of evangelism are passive receivers of a pre-planned presentation of the gospel. Personal evangelism then becomes a way to present a sales pitch rather then engaging in meaningful dialogue focused on the hearer's concern. A second problem with this method is that it uses a cookie-cutter presentation of the gospel, not allowing the good news to touch people differently.

As Peace pointed out, these standardized presentations of the gospel were often very pre-programmed and unwelcoming. He writes, "Personal evangelism turns out to be impersonal evangelism."[104] Many people who engage in personal evangelistic methods tend to give potential converts answers to questions that they are not asking. Sometimes the means for coming to Christ are made so easy that it fails to take into account the important act of the seeker actively searching for the narrow gate. Darius Salter explains this:

> Evangelicals may be far too eager to erase the unruly elements of the conversion process, while packaging the gospel for easy, rapid, and strain-free consumption. Such cognitive reductionism means that the "spiritual" aspects of evangelical life are increasingly approached by means of and interpreted in terms of

---

[104] Richard V. Peace, 293.

principles, rules, steps, laws, codes, guidelines, and so forth.[105]

Salter further points out that "a uniformity of process quite often aims at a uniformity of product, while ignoring the uniqueness of the individual and the varieties of religious experiences."[106] Joseph C. Aldrich criticized this type of outreach, calling it confrontational/intrusional evangelism. He points out that while this is a legitimate method of evangelism, it only reaches a small percentage of people.

> Most evangelism training programs focus their training upon a confrontational approach to evangelism. However, it is naïve to assume that the majority of people trust Christ as a result of a stranger witnessing to them during a one-time spiritual transaction. The vast majority do *not* become Christians by confrontational, stranger-to-stranger evangelism. Furthermore, many are being kept from making an effective decision because of bad experiences with a zealous but insensitive witness. Much of the problem grows out of some false assumptions about the decision-making process.[107]

In the 1980s, the distaste that some Christians felt toward this confrontational type of evangelism resulted in a modification of personal evangelism to an approach called "lifestyle" evangelism. Lifestyle evangelism, or friendship evangelism, encourages Christians to build relationships outside the church community to win people to Christ. Aldrich, a proponent of lifestyle evangelism describes it as incarnational/relational evangelism accomplished through the steps of presence, proclamation, and persuasion. According to Aldrich, "a

---

[105] Salter, 208–209.
[106] Ibid., 209.
[107] Joseph C. Aldrich, *Life-Style Evangelism: Crossing Traditional Boundaries to Reach the Unbelieving World* (Portland, OR: Multnomah Press, 1981), 79.

Christian becomes good news as Christ ministers through his serving heart. As his friends hear the music of the gospel (presence) they become predisposed to respond to its words (proclamation) and then hopefully are persuaded to act (persuasion)."[108]

This non-confrontational style of evangelism is not without its problems. One is that those who practice it tend to be a little too non-confrontational. Paige Patterson writes, "The most telling critique of lifestyle evangelism, as far as evangelicals are concerned, is the criticism that the New Testament apparently sanctions a more aggressive and confrontational approach."[109]

Another problem is the motive for developing friendships. Richard Peace notes that "the biggest problem with lifestyle evangelism, however, was developing friendships with non-Christians. Aldrich (and others) points out that many Christians do not have meaningful relationships with anyone but Christians. This raises the whole question of motives for friendship."[110] Becoming friends with people with an ulterior motive to convert them to Christ goes against every grain of integrity and ethics that makes for true friendship.

Media evangelism is another kind of encounter evangelism, but differs from mass evangelism in that the evangelist is connected to the audience by electronic media. Radio was the first electronic medium used to reach the masses, followed by television and film. Today, with internet and technology so readily available, the gospel can easily be presented to everyone in the world who is connected to media. Jan J. van Capelleveen commented at the World Congress on Evangelism in Berlin in 1966,

> As never before we must update our magazines, our radio broadcasts, our television programs, our firms, and our books. Compare the literature of the past century with that of ours. Tears, either of joy or sorrow, fell on every other page. There were involved

---

[108] Ibid., 81.
[109] Paige Patterson, *Lifestyle Evangelism,* ed. Thom S. Rainer, *Evangelism in the Twenty-First Century* (Wheaton, IL: Harold Shaw Publishers, 1989), 43.
[110] Richard V. Peace, 294.

sentences and lengthy descriptions. Now our books are full of hard facts, succinct sentences—and you might never know whether the hero had brown or blue eyes. But many religious editors still use the style and the lay-out and the verbosity of yesteryear. Do we realize that a picture is worth a thousand words, that an art editor is worth four copywriters? That white spaces are sometimes more important for readability than the words we use? We need more professionals, or we will be communicating only with the wastebasket.[111]

Since the congress in Berlin, evangelicals have increasingly embraced and promoted the use of mass media to share the story of the gospel. Major evangelistic movies have been released in local theatres and Christian radio and television stations have emerged as an accepted means of reaching the lost. The increase in Christian internet ministries is another indication that Christians are embracing cutting-edge technology to cross borders with the gospel. However, media evangelism is not without its limitations. One is that it is, under-standably, impersonal and too general in its gospel presentation. It primarily touches those who are at a crisis point in their lives, desperate for hope, and ready to respond to Jesus. Media evangelism or any other type of evangelism has little impact on those who are not looking for Jesus.

The problem with encounter evangelism in the forms of mass evangelism, personal evangelism, lifestyle evangelism, and media evangelism is that not everyone who hears the gospel during an encounter is at a crisis point in their lives in which they are ready to respond to Jesus. People who are not prepared to receive Christ either reject the idea of someone trying to convert them or need time to consider what they have heard through encounter evangelism.

---

[111] Jan J. Van Capelleveen "Evangelism and Communication," in *One Race One Gospel One Task* eds. Carl F. Henry and W. Stanley Mooneyham, (Minneapolis, MN: World Wide Publications, 1967), 302–303.

Encounter evangelism has brought some to Christ, but in reality it has failed to produce many disciples. It was a legitimate way of reaching out to people, but not the most effective way.

Process Evangelism

Richard Peace identified four types of outreach that are considered process evangelism: small-group evangelism, growth-oriented evangelism, evangelism via spiritual disciplines, and worship evangelism. Unlike encounter evangelism, process evangelism focuses more on specific issues and specific audiences than on a general gospel with no precise target audience. In process evangelism, the activities tend to be carried out on a smaller scale than mass events. Whereas encounter evangelism is a special activity with a particular methodology, process evangelism is a philosophy and practice intended to permeate all aspects of the Christian life.

Peace identifies small groups as the major setting for process evangelism, pointing out that among the variety of methods of evangelism used today, "Still, the most effective witness so often springs from the *community* of believers. Today, some of the deepest and most significant witness occurs when a small group of Christians and non-Christians meet together to discuss Christianity."[112] Large churches like Willow Creek and Saddleback have embraced small groups as entry points into the church for many seekers. In its small groups, Willow Creek encourages the use of the open chair concept, in which an empty chair is visible during each meeting as a reminder of the community's responsibility to reach out. Willow Creek states, "The picture of the open chair represents the desire in the church to assimilate and include new people into the group structure ... Some groups are prepared to receive seekers. In such cases group leaders and members must be sensitive to the needs and spiritual maturity level of a seeker."[113]

---

[112] Richard Peace, *Small Group Evangelism: A Training Program for Reaching Out with the Gospel* (Downers Grove, IL: InterVarsity Press, 1985), 66.
[113] Bill Donahue, *The Willow Creek Guide to Leading Life-Changing Small Groups* (Grand Rapids, MI: Zondervan Publishing House, 1996), 30.

The strength of the small group structure for evangelism is that it allows people to engage in the process rather than being recipients of a one-way gospel presentation. Dee Brestin writes, "Sometimes we evangelicals legalistically insist that Christians be able to name the date and time of their new birth. Not every one can, but that does not mean they have not been born again."[114]

Another vehicle for process evangelism is growth-oriented groups that focus on an issue of interest to the community to allow believers in a church to connect with community members with the same interest. Among the topics discussed are dealing with everyday life problems, such as marital issues, raising children, and dealing with addictions. Peace describes the value of these discussions: "Sometimes the outreach of choice will involve tackling head-on the issues that trouble people. For each of us as we go through life, problems emerge that cause great distress. Oftentimes hidden in these problems are keys to our spiritual progress."[115] Some growth groups center on personal interests such as learning to paint. Howard Clinebell writes, "Churches should play a strategic part in the growth network needed to develop the unused human potentialities in every community."[116] The thinking is that eventually, the spiritual component surfaces and the relationship between strangers develops to the point where participants feel safe about discussing related personal spiritual matters.

A third type of process evangelism is evangelism through the teaching of spiritual disciplines in an attempt to respond to the increasing interest in spiritual matters in this postmodern era. Every year, people spend billions on books, videos, seminars, and retreats concerning various forms of spirituality, from Christian to New Age. In Christian circles, much interest has been shown in spiritual journaling, *lectio divina,* and meditative prayer. Because people outside the church are interested in these matters, teaching on them provides an oppor-tunity for Christians to try and reach those seeking spirituality. Peace points out that

---

[114] Dee Brestin, *Finders Keepers: Introducing Your Friends to Christ and Helping Them Grow* (Wheaton, IL: Harold Shaw Publishers, 1983), 134.
[115] Richard V. Peace, 336.
[116] Howard John Clinebell, *Growth Groups* (Nashville: Abingdon, 1977), 128.

It makes sense for the church to institute programs that enable people to get in touch with spirituality, both its concepts and its practices. And these programs need to be made accessible and attractive to people outside the church. This is a direct form of process evangelism. Such programs need to be characterized by exploration of various approaches to spirituality, by immersion in the actual practices themselves, and by focused discussion concerning the God one seeks to connect with by means of such practices.[117]

One example of using spiritual disciplines in process evangelism is the catechism course that G. I. Williamson, a reformed Presbyterian, has developed for his church in New Zealand. His approach is also an example of using a systematic approach to teach Christian truths as a way of reaching people for Christ. Williamson used a catechism course because he believes that "there is a *system* of doctrine taught in the Bible."[118] Church history shows that the Methodist movement developed a systematic method of disciples making that could be described as a form of pre-discipleship. Robert Coleman describes this process:

Anyone desiring salvation from sins could become a Methodist. But this desire, as Wesley noted, "must be evidenced by three marks: Avoiding all known sin; doing good after his power; and, attending all the ordinances of God." This involved participating in a small class meeting each week, where Methodist discipline was enforced. These informal gatherings were ideally suited to personal fears and needs, and

---

[117] Ibid., 340–341.
[118] G. I. Williamson, *The Shorter Catechism,* (Phillipsburg, NJ: Presbyterian and Reformed Publishing Co., 1978), *v.*

for this reason they probably contributed more to the growth of the church than any other program.[119]

An even earlier example of teaching spirituality to seekers of the faith are the catechumenate classes of the early church, which, as has been described, involved providing teaching and instruction before believers were asked to consider accepting Christ. John Morgan-Wynne describes the relationship between instruction of converts and baptism:

> Now the act of baptism appears to have followed immediately on the act of believing, the commitment to Christ, conversion, certainly in the early days of Christian movement, as Acts reflects that story. Early teaching for converts seems to presuppose the act of baptism, in its stress on the need to go on putting off evil habits and wrong attitudes.[120]

Worship evangelism, a fourth practice of process evangelism, is growing in popularity because supporters think the worship experience can be a powerful way for seekers to begin to understand the dynamics of God. Robert Webber, who calls this approach liturgical evangelism, writes, "liturgical evangelism calls a person into Christ and the church through a conversion regulated and ordered by worship. These services order the inner experience of repentance from sin, faith in Christ, conversion of life, and entrance into the Christian community."[121]

In worship evangelism, seekers can attend church and be part of a Christian community before making any kind of commitment to Christ. Daniel Benedict and Craig Miller see worship as precatechesis and catechesis.

---

[119] Robert E. Coleman, *"Nothing to Do but To Save Souls"; John Wesley's Charge to His Preachers* (Grand Rapids, MI: Francis Asbury Press, 1990), 35.

[120] John E. Morgan-Wynne, "References To Baptism in the Fourth Gospel," eds. Stanley E. Porter and Anthony R. Cross, *Baptism, The New Testament and the Church* (Sheffield: Sheffield Academic Press, 1999), 125.

[121] Robert E. Webber, *Liturgical Evangelism* (Harrisburg, PA: Morehouse Publishing, 1986), 1.

> Precatechesis and catechesis are the sum total of those processes that allow for the Word of God to echo or resound in the mind, heart, and life of persons. Precatechesis aims at informing and interpreting the gospel. Catechesis aims at formation and conversion to the gospel. Both are first and foremost the work of God in Christ by the Spirit, and only by vocation, your work and that of your congregation.[122]

Worship evangelism becomes a process in which some of the lost are being reached through the spiritual life of the church.

While both encounter evangelism and process evangelism have their strengths and weaknesses, process evangelism seems to fit the disciple-making aspect of the Great Commission better. Encounter evangelism reaches only a segment of society and is ineffective in connecting with those who are dealing with specific issues and need a more personal touch. Process evangelism is more relational, addressing the yearning for spiritual relationships and community in the postmodern world. As the church moves more from encounter evangelism to process evangelism, the use of catechetical instruction may again become more prominent in evangelism. This practice of process evangelism includes pre-discipleship in its outreach.

RETHINKING EVANGELISM

Since current definitions of evangelism contain the idea of making disciples, our outreach strategies and practices need to have this discipleship component. Effective evangelism must lead into discipleship. The work of the evangelist is not only to bring a lost one to Christ, but also to maturity. The work of the evangelist must involve a teaching

---

[122] Daniel T. Benedict and Craig Kennet Miller, *Contemporary Worship for the 21st Century: Worship or Evangelism?* (Nashville: Discipleship Resources, 1994, reprint 2001), 43.

component in pre-discipleship, which leads to discipleship. This means that the pre-discipleship process needs to be part of evangelism.

The overview of today's encounter and process evangelism reveals that traditional evangelistic efforts are not as effective as the church would like to them to be. This leads to a need for us to rethink our strategies for evangelism. Evangelism must move toward that which is personal and informative through a pre-discipleship process.

The suggestion to incorporate pre-discipleship into the evangelistic process is not saying that we remove everything we do in evangelism and start from scratch. We do many things well in evangelism. The meetings, presentations, music, drama, and many other forms of evangelistic efforts have been done to the highest degree of excellence. Many of the events and meetings I have attended were very professional in nature and glorifying to God. On the one hand, we should continue to pray, preach, share, and evangelize as we have done before, but on the other hand we need to re-evaluate the way we invite people to Jesus. Rather than asking people to make a commitment to Christ and trying to manipulate them into some kind of decision when they are not ready, we need to ask them if they are ready to come to Christ. If they are not ready, we should present them with the option to discover Christ over time.

For example, at an evangelistic meeting after all the prayers, drama, music, testimonies, and preaching, we come to that moment of commitment. At that moment of invitation, we have often given seekers a choice to embrace Christ or reject Christ. History shows us that less than five percent of the people in many of these evangelistic meetings embrace Christ. The majority of seekers in these evangelistic meetings are not ready to receive or reject Christ. We need to give them a third option to discover Christ.

This third option allows us to introduce a pre-discipleship process into our evangelistic efforts. It recognizes that not all seekers are ready to embrace Christ during the invitation and need time to process the gospel. The option relieves the pressure for the seeker to make an unprepared commitment and opens a way for further study and examination of Christianity. In this renewed philosophy of evangelism, converts through the pre-discipleship process have the opportunity to make a sound, intelligent, and emotionally balanced commitment to Christ that leads to a willing life of discipleship.

In conclusion, the church needs to take a fresh approach to making disciples. Many of today's evangelistic efforts are ineffective and the church needs an alternative approach, which opens the door to pre-discipleship. Pre-discipleship is part of the work of the evangelist and can fill a need as the church moves from encounter evangelism to process evangelism. Pre-discipleship is the catechumenal study needed in contemporary evangelism.

CHAPTER SIX:

PRE-DISCIPLESHIP IN CONVERSION

In Mark 10, Jesus was leaving Jericho when Bartimaeus, a blind man, cried out to him. After some interactions, Jesus healed Bartimaeus and he received his sight immediately. Another time, in John 9, Jesus saw a man blind from his birth. After some discussion with his disciples, Jesus spat on the ground, made some mud with the saliva, and put it on the man's eye. He then told the blind man to go wash in the Pool of Sioam. When the man went and washed, he returning home seeing. In Mark 8, Jesus was introduced to a blind man at Bethsaida. Jesus took the man by the hand outside the village and spat on the man's eyes. The man did not see clearly at first, but he did see clearly after a second touch from Jesus. Jesus healed all three blind men, yet all three blind men received their sight differently. In the same way, the spiritually blind receive their sight differently.

An understanding of the process of conversion lends credibility to effective evangelism. We must first define conversion and understand that there are different models of conversion. We need to understand the changes that occur in conversion, especially through the theological and psychological lens. Evangelicals must understand conversion as a process that occurs over time, affecting change cognitively, emotively, and volitionally. This conversion process will be seen to support the need for a pre-discipleship model in evangelism.

Today many Christians regard conversion, the change from a sinful life to accepting Christ, as a sudden, instantaneous decision, as though the convert were crossing an imaginary spiritual line into eternal life. In this view, which is often based on the experience of the Apostle Paul on the Damascus road, conversion is a dramatic and unforgettable experience. However, while this is not the only a model of conversion, it can create problems in the Christian community. The dramatic conversion as the model of conversion that is most widely held. Many Christians who only know of the Apostle Paul's model of conversion have become confused when their conversion experiences were not like that of the Apostle. Some who grew up in Christian homes had less dramatic experiences of conversion in becoming followers of Jesus. Those conversions, however, are as valid as those who had a dramatic experience. What then is conversion? How should Christians understand it?

DEFINITION OF CONVERSION

The biblical meaning of conversion is "turning" and to convert means "to turn." The Hebrew word in the Old Testament for conversion, שׁוּב (shub), which means "to turn, return, restore, bring back" is found more than a thousand times, mostly in the context of turning from evil and returning to the Lord. Conversion in the Old Testament had the sense of returning to where you were, remembering that you belong to the Lord, and of wandering no more in idolatry and sin.

The Greek words in the New Testament for conversion, μετάνοια and ἐπιστροφή, mean "to turn around." According to Kittel, μετάνοια means to "change one's mind," "change of mind," "to convert," or "conversion." ἐπιστροφή means "to convert," or "to change (someone)."[123] Kittel pointed out that "the terms have religious and ethical significance along the lines of the OT and Jewish concept of conversion, for which there is no analogy in secular Greek."[124] It has the idea of stopping and proceeding in a new direction. The key understanding in the New Testament of conversion is as a change in direction. Jim Wallis accents the changes that occur in conversion:

> In the biblical narratives, the "from" and "to" of
> conversion are usually quite clear. Conversion is

---

[123] Kittel, 722.
[124] Kittel, 999.

from sin to salvation, from idols to God, from slavery to freedom, from injustice to justice, from guilt to forgiveness, from lies to truth, from darkness to light, from self to others, from death to life, and much more. Conversion always means to turn to God. But what it means to turn to God is both universal and particular to each historical situation. We are called to respond to God always in the particulars of our own personal, social, and political circumstances. But conversion is also universal: it entails a reversal of the historical givens whatever they may be at any place and time.[125]

Yet, while the meaning of conversion is clear theologically, the actual process of conversion is not as straightforward to describe as many would like it to be, because the conversion process can occur in a number of ways. Richard Peace argues that the substance of conversion is much more important than the experience of conversion itself.

Human beings have the ability to undergo remarkable transformations of a cognitive, affective, behavioural, social, and religious nature that seem to tip their lives upside down and launch them in whole new and positive directions. This is an important observation since it means that *the essence of conversion is not found in the experience itself but in the content of that experience.* In the work of ministry, the question then must be: In conversion, from what to whom has a person turned? The question is not: What is the shape of that person's experience, and does it conform to what we consider a normative exper-

---

[125] Jim Wallis, *The Call To Conversion: Why Faith Is Always Personal But Never Private* (San Francisco: Harper & Row, Publishers, 1981), 5–6.

ience? But even with this qualification, the question still remains: What is genuine conversion?[126]

In reality, the Christian conversion experience can be understood in different ways, depending on the context, as Kasdorf observes:

> Depending on the culture and social structure within which man lives, the conversion experience may be that of a people movement by caste, clan, tribe, or family making decisions by multi-personal actions; or it may be that of the individual persons who independently and irrespectively of others, turn one by one from sin to forgiveness. The various case stories illustrate from actual life experiences how the different types and ways estranged and separated sinners convert and become reconciled people of God.[127]

THE KINDS OF CONVERSIONS

In an attempt to define genuine conversion, the questions that Walter Conn raises about the conversion process keep surfacing: "Are conversions sudden events or gradual processes? Is conversion a single, once-and-for-all event in a person's life? Or may a person experience two, three, or more conversions at different points in life?"[128] The literature indicates that not all conversions occur as a once-and-for-all event, but for many Christians can take the form of a gradual process. Conversions need to be seen through different models as people are being saved in different ways. This may result in differing models for evangelism.

In his study of the psychology of religion, Raymond Paloutzian identifies three models of conversion in traditional religion and the

---

[126] Richard V. Peace, 6–7.
[127] Ibid., 25–26.
[128] Walter Conn, *Christian Conversion* (New York: Paulist Press, 1986), 9.

reasons for them: the sudden conversion, the unconscious conversion, and the gradual conversion. Paloutzian states that "the most dramatic of the conversion types is the sudden conversion. Here the conversion occurs all at once, on the 'spur of the moment.'"[129] The sudden conversion is the type Apostle Paul experienced in which it occurred in a short time span and was dramatically emotional. Paloutzian argues, "certain people are predisposed to sudden conversion because intrapersonal conflicts and frustrations (e.g., feelings of personal inadequacy, lack of self-worth, guilt over a misdeed) have been repressed."[130]

At the other end of the spectrum is the unconscious conversion, in which people who have grown up with the faith cannot recall a time when they made a conscious decision to believe in Christ. Such was the case of Timothy, who learned of the Holy Scripture from infancy (2 Timothy 3:15). Often, unconscious converts are not troubled by repressed conflict or personal frustrations as is the sudden convert. According to Paloutzian, unconscious converts are influenced by the social learning reinforcement and modeling that they received at home and take a lifetime to embrace their beliefs.

Gradual conversion, the third type that Paloutzian identified, involves the convert taking a period of time, ranging from a few days to a few years, to make a commitment to Christ. Paloutzian found that gradual converts were conscious of their conflict and frustration, had a cognitive need for answers, and searched the various belief systems to which they were exposed. The Bereans are biblical examples of gradual converts; they *"examined the Scriptures every day to see if what Paul said was true"* (Acts 17:11). The gradual convert is more likely to go through an intellectual type of process of conversion, which Paloutzian describes.

Psychological explanations of gradual conversion imply a more intellectual type of process than either

---

[129]Raymond F. Paloutzian, *Invitation to the Psychology of Religion* (Glenview, IL: Scott, Foresman and Company, 1983), 110.
[130] Ibid.

of the other two types of conversion. Theoretically, gradual converts may experience conflict and frustration, but these are not repressed as they are in sudden conversion. Rather, the person makes conscious efforts to resolve them. The conflicts might be personal, societal, and religious values; or the frustration might be due to a discrepancy between the person's actual desired levels of performance in the moral or intellectual sphere.[131]

Others, such as Richard Peace, also support the concept of conversion as being a process rather than a line that is crossed:

> A proper biblical understanding of conversion (derived from the seminal experience of St. Paul) will enable us to understand in a new way how the Twelve came to faith. The assumption in Biblical studies seems to be (though few address the question) that the act of joining Jesus' apostolic band was equivalent to their conversion. But was this the case? Were they converted at the moment they responded to Jesus' invitation to become fishers of men? Or did conversion take place when they were commissioned as apostles? Perhaps it took place when they affirmed that Jesus was indeed the Messiah. Or did it occur at the moment of the miracle of the second touch? In fact, on the basis of the understanding derived from Paul's experience, none of these experiences would qualify as the moment of conversion. Instead, each played a vital part in the final experience of conversion.[132]

---

[131] Paloutzian., 111–112.
[132] Richard V. Peace, 12–13.

Joost De Blank, the former Anglican archbishop of Cape Town, South Africa, points out that the process of conversion is the work of God and primarily the work of the Holy Spirit.

> The act of conversion marks a beginning—but only a beginning. It makes the convert "accepted in the Beloved"; and as a result he is admitted as a member of Christ's family. But justification is a cold and bleak state to be in—like a baby born only to be exposed and left to die. We need always to remember that the act of Conversion is fundamentally the work of God. It is *His action* in which we fully take our share, and it is primarily the work of the Holy Spirit actively engaged in the hearts of men ... Our salvation is wrought through the work of the Spirit the Sanctifier, and therefore it is through him that our Conversion is being increasing effected.[133]

The Holy Spirit is actively involved in the process of conversion and his work is ongoing, as Jesus explained.

> "When he comes, he will convict the world of guilt in regard to sin and righteousness and judgment: in regard to sin, because men do not believe in me; in regard to righteousness, because I am going to the Father, where you can see me no longer; and in regard to judgment, because the prince of this world now stands condemned. I have much more to say to you, more than you can now bear. But when he, the Spirit of truth, comes, he will guide you into all truth." (John 16:8-13a)

---

[133] Joost De Blank, *This Is Conversion* (London: Hodder and Stoughton, 1957, reprint 1961), 50–51.

It is the Holy Spirit who first convicts people of sin and guides them into all truth. He influences and ultimately indwells believers, teaching about and leading them toward eternal life. Conversion is a process that takes time, energy, and effort in the individual and the witnesses of the gospel in cooperation with the work of the Holy Spirit.

In light of what Paloutzian and others say about conversion being a process, it seems appropriate for the church to evaluate its approach to evangelism after focusing so intently on sudden conversion. Pre-discipleship is a practice that would meet the need of those requiring time to consider the Christian truth while experiencing conversion as a process.

THE CHANGES IN CONVERSION

An understanding of the nature of change in conversion will help Christians to rethink methods of outreach and discipleship, especially in relation to the gradual form of conversion that many people experience. One source of information is the psychological models for conversion. Most of them, like most theological models, have understood conversion as a process. It is prudent to understand conversion through the science of the mind. A healthy examination of conversion through a psychological lens will aid in the understanding of how the mind changes in the process of conversion. Cedric B. Johnson and H. Newton Malony discuss the need for study on the process of conversion:

> Psychologists and biblical theologians describe the decision of the converting person as a process that brings new direction. The process begins with an awareness of God and in a later stage finds the person incorporated into the church. The new direction is evident in a turn from one faith toward Christ. Post-conversion beliefs and behaviors coincide to a large extent with those of the person's new community. To what extent can these behaviors be predicted? How extensive is the change in the life of the new convert?

The psychological research on personality change
and conversion is inconclusive. Standard personality
measures do not seem to ask the right questions. Is it
purely an outward change or does conversion have
inward subjective elements?[134]

The patriarch of psychology, William James, identifies two
changes that occur in the mind in the process of conversion:

> To begin with, there are two things in the mind of the
> candidate for conversion: first, the present incomp-
> leteness or wrongness, the "sin" which he is eager to
> escape from; and second, the positive ideal which he
> longs to compass. Now with most of us the sense of
> our present wrongness is a far more distinct piece of
> our consciousness than is the imagination of any
> positive ideal we can aim at. In a majority of cases,
> indeed, the "sin" almost exclusively engrosses the
> attention, so that conversion is a *"process of
> struggling away from sin rather than of striving
> towards righteousness."*[135]

In their study of religious conversion, Joe Edward Barnhart and
Mary Ann Barnhart describe the changes needed for a conversion to
occur. They identify three dimensions of religious conversion, the
psychological, the social, and the cultural, and identify the
psychological in "at least three modes in which the sense of rock-
bottom finitude manifests itself. They are the moral, the emotional, and
the intellectual or cognitive."[136] The Barnharts also identify the social
aspect of conversion, in which "the individual must learn to live outside

---

[134] Cedric B. Johnson and H. Newton Malony, *Christian Conversion: Biblical and
Psychological Perspectives* (Grand Rapids, MI: Zondervan Publishing House, 1982),
111.
[135] William James, *The Varieties of Religious Experience: A Study in Human Nature*
(New York: Vintage Books, 1990), 194.
[136] Joe Edward Barnhart and Mary Ann Barnhart, *The New Birth: A Naturalistic View of
Religious Conversion* (Macon, GA: Mercer University Press, 1981), 24.

his mother's biological womb, but he cannot live outside the new social womb. It is the social womb that prevents him from becoming totally mad and destroyed by the terror of chaos and finitude shock."[137] The third dimension of conversion the Barnharts identify is the cultural, which varies depending on the context of this pluralistic society. The significance of the Barnharts' understanding of conversion to this thesis is that the process of conversion is multi-faceted.

Peter Masters, senior pastor of the Metropolitan Tabernacle in London and author of *Physician of Souls,* has been influenced by the Reformed and Wesleyan understanding of *Ordo Salutis* (order of salvation) in describing the changes that occur in conversion. Masters, who believes that faith and repentance follow the grace that is granted through the Holy Spirit, writes about the five stages of conversion, describing each as the anatomy and order of conversion. These five stages are the conception stage, the awakened and convicted stage, the repentance and faith stage, the justification and the new birth stage, and the sealed and assured stage.

Masters views "conception," which he calls the first stage, as an act of God in regeneration. Masters points out that "the Word of God uses the illustration of birth, because the *whole birth process* is a picture of a man's salvation. Can there be a birth without there first being a conception?"[138] In this stage, people begin to feel the void within, their lack of peace, and need for spirituality. This leads to the second stage, the awakened and convicted stage, in which people are conscious of their guilt and aware of their failure and shame before God. This is the stage where the person is confronted with the word of God and the gospel and challenged with the call to repent and believe.

Repentance and faith are the third stage of conversion, the one in which people choose to willingly trust in Jesus as their saviour and follow him as Lord in repentance and faith. The next stage is justification and the new birth, in which God declares that the sinner is now pardoned, clean, just, and righteous through the atoning blood of Jesus Christ. Simultaneously, the sinner is also spiritually born again.

---

[137] Ibid., 82.
[138] Peter Masters, *Physician of Souls* (London: Wakeman Publishers Ltd., 1976), 83.

At the same time, in the last stage of the sealing of assurance, and possibly an immediate advanced level of assurance, the new believer feels the assurance from God concerning his or her salvation through the sealing of the Holy Spirit. Masters says that only two of these stages take time while the others are instantaneous.

> Once conception has occurred the next stage is the awakening and conviction of the sinner; after which come (instantly) justification and the new birth ... it must be stressed that the only stages which may be drawn out over a period of time are stages (2) and (3)—*Awakening and Conviction* and *Repentance and Faith.* Once repentance and faith are accomplished, everything else is instant.[139]

Like Masters, Richard Peace divides the conversion process in stages. However, he identifies three main things that occur in genuine conversion: insight, turning, and transformation. The insight is the cognitive understanding about God and self that occurs before repentance. Converts must understand that they are sinners before a holy God before they can be saved. The turning is the turning from sin and a hardened heart to Jesus Christ as Saviour and Lord. The third aspect of Peace's conversion model is transformation, which involves forgiveness, discipleship, and a new life.

> There are insight, turning, and transformation that affect who he is, how he relates to Jesus, and what he does within his culture. Furthermore, these movements within these spheres are all in the context of God. Christian conversion is not a generalized movement of transformation within the context of one's relationships to other people and to the world around one. It involves new insight into God, new turning toward God, and a new life lived in response to God.

---

[139] Ibid., 88.

> It involves seeing oneself in the light of God's truth, embracing a new relationship to God, and living this out within the community of God's people as a servant and witness to all people.[140]

James Fowler, a pioneer in the work of faith development, created a model that has six stages of faith, which provides further insight into an understanding of conversion. Fowler, who uses a model of stages of human development, begins with the infant stage, in which the person has an undifferentiated faith. Once infants begin to use thought and language, opening themselves up to the use of symbols in speech and ritual play, they begin to transition into the first stage of faith.

Fowler's first stage of faith was intuitive-projective faith, which relates to the intuitive-projective child, whose age is between two to six. Children in this stage use speech and symbolic representation to arrange their sensory experience into meaning units and "they simply assume without question that the experiences and perceptions they have of a phenomenon represent the only available perspective."[141] This is the stage in which children, ages two to six, believe that Santa Claus is real and faith is simple. It is the kind of child-like faith that Jesus embraced (Matthew 18:3).

The second stage of faith, according to Fowler, is the mythic-literal, in which children, age seven to twelve, try to sort out what is real to what is make-believe. In this stage, older children can share their experiences in story form, so the narrative form of communication is an effective medium to share the gospel with this child.

Fowler's third stage of faith is synthetic-conventional faith, in which adolescents are draped with a new burden of self-consciousness. Because of this, adolescents begin conforming their beliefs to their own identity.

---

[140] Richard Peace, 101.
[141] James W. Fowler, *Stages of Faith: The Psychology of Human Development and the Quest for Meaning* (San Francisco: Harper Collins Publishers, 1981), 123.

God—when God remains or becomes salient in a person's faith at this stage—must also be re-imaged as having inexhaustible depths and as being capable of knowing personally those mysterious depths of self and others we know that we ourselves will never know. Much of the extensive literature about adolescent conversion can be illumined, I believe, by the recognition that the adolescent's religious hunger is for a God who knows, accepts and confirms the self deeply, and who serves as an infinite guarantor of the self with its forming myth of personal identity and faith.[142]

Between the third and fourth stage, Fowler recognizes a transition in which people move from total independence on external authority to relocating the authority for their lives to themselves. The fourth stage of faith according to Fowler is what he terms individuative-reflective faith. This stage takes form mainly in young adulthood, which could range from the twenties to mid-thirties, and even into the forties. This is the stage in which a person begins to "take seriously the burden of responsibility for his or her own commitments, lifestyle, beliefs, and attitudes … this is a 'demythologizing' stage. It is likely to attend minimally to unconscious factors influencing its judgments and behavior."[143]

The next stage of faith, according to Fowler, is conjunctive faith. This stage often occurs at mid-life when people begin to see the validity of other systems of belief, and resolves the paradoxes they have been wrestling with in the previous stage. Fowler writes concerning conjunctive faith:

What the previous stage struggled to clarify, in terms of the boundaries of self and outlook, this stage now makes porous and permeable. Alive to paradox and

---

[142] Fowler, 153.
[143] Ibid., 182.

the truth in apparent contradictions, this stage strives to unify opposites in mind and experience. It generates and maintains vulnerability to the strange truths of those who are "other." Ready for closeness to that which is different and threatening to self and outlook (including new depths of experience in spirituality and religious revelation), this stage's commitment to justice is freed from the confines of tribe, class, religious community or nation.[144]

The sixth stage of faith is universalizing faith, which Fowler says is rare. In this stage, people have lived out the conjunctive stage to perfection and have learned to transcend conflicting loyalties. This does not mean that people at this stage are perfect, but rather that they reflect and model that ultimate development in the faith journey. In this stage, people display "leadership initiatives, often involving strategies of nonviolent suffering and ultimate respect for being, constitute affronts to our usual notions of relevance."[145] They become selfless martyrs for what they believe.

Fowler says that conversion, which is a matter of changing the contents of faith, can occur at any stage of faith. "Conversion is a significant recentering of one's previous conscious or unconscious images of value and power, and the conscious adoption of a new set of master stories in the commitment to reshape one's life in a new community of interpretation and action."[146]

Another psychologist, Jane Loevinger, theorizes a seven-stage model of ego development as a process that forms moral judgment, character, and conscience in people. Loevinger's analysis of ego development also supports the idea that life itself is a process of changes. Although her ego development is more of a psychological analysis of the changes of life, it parallels James Fowler's stages of faith. She begins with a pre-stage call the pre-social, which parallels

---

[144] Ibid., 198.
[145] Ibid., 200.
[146] Ibid., 281–282.

Fowler's pre-stage of undifferentiated faith of the infant. The first stage of ego development is the symbolic stage, in which the baby begins to use language as a sense of being a separate person, while the second stage is the impulsive stage, in which children's impulses allow them to affirm their separate identity. These two stages of ego development parallel Fowler's intuitive-projective stage of faith.[147]

The third stage of ego development is the self-protective stage, in which a child has a corresponding vulnerability, guardedness, and self-centeredness, and is therefore self-protective. The fourth stage is the conformist stage, which parallels Fowler's synthetic-conventional stage of faith development. People in this stage are seeking approval and belonging from family members and peers while judging others on the externals of life.

In the transition from the fourth to the fifth stage is the self-aware level at which people become sensitive to their inner life and failings. The fifth stage in Loevinger's model is the conscientious stage. "At the conscientious stage, the major elements of an adult conscience are present. They include long-term, self-evaluated goals and ideals, differentiated self-criticism, and a sense of responsibility."[148] At this stage, there is also an individualistic level of ego development that deals with issues of tolerance, emotional dependence, relationships, responsibilities, goals, and psychological development.

The sixth stage of Loevinger's ego development is the autonomous stage, in which people accept inner conflict and the complexity of reality. They are free from rigid conscience and cherish individuality and relationships; they begin to value self-fulfillment over achievement. This sixth stage parallels Fowler's conjunctive stage of faith development. The seventh stage is the integrated stage, which Loevinger saw as the highest, representing the perfection of the auto-nomous stage. "For the most part, the description of the Autonomous Stage holds also for the Integrated Stage. A new element is consol-

---

[147] Appendix 1.
[148] Jane Loevinger, *Ego Development: Conceptions and Theories* (San Francisco: Jossey-Bass Publishers, 1976), 20.

idation of a sense of identity. Probably the best description of this stage is that of Maslow's Self-Actualizing person."[149]

Loevinger's model of ego development and Fowler's model of faith development became the foundation of Daniel Helminiak's model for spiritual development, which is significant for understanding some of the changes that occur in the conversion process. Helminiak believed that spiritual development in human development is mainly an adult phenomenon and that this development began in late adolescence or early adulthood. He writes, "It is clear, then, that not chronological age but level of development defines what is meant by the 'adult' nature of spiritual development. For spiritual development is proper to the self-responsible subject."[150]

Helminiak begins by saying that the starting point of spiritual development is the conformist stage and uses Loevinger's fourth stage of ego development, the conformist stage, and Fowler's third stage of faith development, the synthetic-conventional stage, in his model of spiritual development. According to him, this stage is "characterized by a deeply felt and extensively rationalized worldview; accepted on the basis of external authority and supported by approval of one's significant others."[151]

Helminiak's second stage of spiritual development is the conscientious conformist stage, which parallels Loevinger's self-aware level and the transition between Fowler's third and fourth stages of faith development. At this stage, people begin to understand the world and their responses in taking responsibility for their life and the world around them; they also decide what they will make of themselves.

The third stage of Helminiak's spiritual development model is the conscientious stage, in which people do significant restructuring of their lives from conformity to their known world toward their new understanding of the things around them. They are also optimistic about their faith because of a renewed understanding of the world. This stage

---

[149] Ibid., 26.
[150] Daniel A. Helminiak, *Spiritual Development: An Interdisciplinary Study* (Chicago: Loyola University Press, 1987), 79.
[151] Ibid., 85.

parallels Loevinger's conscientious stage and Fowler's individuative-reflective stage.

According to Helminiak, the fourth stage of spiritual development is the compassion stage, which is "characterized by a certain mellowing. Here one learns to surrender some of the world one has so painstakingly constructed for oneself. One's commitments are no less intense, but they are more realistic, more nuanced, and more supported by deeply felt and complex emotion. One becomes more gentle with oneself and with others."[152] This stage parallels Loevinger's autonomous stage and Fowler's conjunctive stage.

Helminiak's final stage of spiritual development is the cosmic stage, which parallels Loevinger's integrated stage and Fowler's universalizing stage. Both Fowler and Loevinger, who approached this stage from a psychological and philosophical point of view, admit they have difficulties describing the last stage. Helminiak suggests that the cosmic stage exists to open new possibilities in development. He views the spiritual development of a human as eternal and something that cannot be finalized in this life. He points out the difficulties of using human standards to measure states like holiness. However, Helminiak did say, "if spiritual development and human development are strict correlates, the 'saints' in any particular historical period or culture would meet the standards of authentic human development current in their historical period or culture; and they would exhibit the same limitations characteristic of their time and place, as well."[153] He concluded that the cosmic stage is being in a state of holiness before the Creator. Helminiak defines holiness as "nothing other than human authenticity recognized as related also to God."[154]

The models of Fowler, Loevinger, and Helminiak explain Paloutzian's idea of unconscious and gradual conversion, while the one developed by James Prochaska explains what happens in those who convert dramatically.

---

[152] Ibid.
[153] Ibid., 87.
[154] Ibid., 149.

Prochaska's model of change shows that there is a way to accelerate the process of change. His transtheoretical model of change argues for five stages of change. The first is the precontemplative stage, in which individuals do not feel any need to change and do not perceive themselves as having problems, regarding problems instead as being external to themselves. The second stage is the contemplative stage, in which individuals begin to recognize that they have problems. In the third or preparation stage, individuals know that they have to change and begin to think and feel that they must take some course of action. In the fourth or action stage, individuals engage in full-scale affirmative actions to overcome their problems. In the fifth or maintenance stage, they make every effort to prevent a recurrence of their problem. Prochaska emphasizes the importance of maintenance:

> There are great challenges at every stage, and maintenance is no exception. For it is during maintenance that you must work to consolidate the gains you attained during the action and other stages, and struggle to prevent lapse and relapse. Change never ends with action. Although traditional therapy sees maintenance as a static stage, in fact it is a critically important continuation that can last from as little as six months to as long as a lifetime.[155]

Prochaska's first four stages of change remarkably parallel Helminiak's first three stages of spiritual development. The maintenance stage in Prochaska's model can be seen in Helminiak's final two stages. Both models of change can be seen as occurring over a long or a short period of time, which is significant in understanding the changes in conversion because both models allow for changes in the dramatic, unconscious, or gradual conversion.

If one applies Prochaska's model of change to Christian conversion, then at the precontemplative stage, the individual feels no need for

---

[155] James O. Prochaska, John C. Norcross, and Carlo C. Diclemente, *Changing For Good* (New York: Avon Books, 1994), 45.

any kind of spiritual life. At the contemplative stage, individuals realize that they have sinned before Almighty God. In the preparation stage, individuals know that they need to do something about that sin and are willing to take action concerning their status with God. The action stage is the act of repentance and the willingness to follow Jesus and embrace the Christian faith. The maintenance stage is discipleship in which people grow toward maturity in their relationship with Jesus Christ.

Motivation also plays a key part in effecting change, and it can take a negative or positive form. When people want to help another to change certain behaviours, for example in clinical counselling, they usually try to motivate them toward change by showing them how they can avoid discomfort, pain, fear, shame, guilt, loss, threat, anxiety, or humiliation. Some evangelicals use these motivational approaches in their gospel presentations, evoking shame, guilt, and fear, which results in some people embracing Christ because of the guilt of sin and anxiety about eternal damnation. However, there are more positive modes of motivations for conversion, which can range from the echoes of love, joy, and peace to the prospect of a deep relationship with the Creator. William Miller and Stephen Rollnick, experts on change in psychological studies, affirm that positive motivations for change are much more constructive than negative motivations.

> Humiliation, shame, guilt, and angst are not the primary engines of change. Ironically, such experiences can even immobilize the person, rendering change more remote. Instead, constructive behavior change seems to arise when the person connects it with something of intrinsic value, something important, something cherished. Intrinsic motivation for change arises in an accepting, empower atmosphere that makes it safe for the person to explore the possibly painful present in relation to what is wanted and valued. People often get stuck, not because they fail to appreciate the down side of their situation, but because they feel at least two ways about it. The way

out of that forest has to do with exploring and following what the person is experiencing and what, from his or her perspective, truly matters.[156]

In summary, the changes in conversion are cognitive, emotive, and volitional. Cognitive changes in conversion have been addressed by Prochaska's model of change. Prochaska's first three stages deal with change on the cognitive level. His fourth stage of change is the action stage in which there is a volitional change. Miller and Rollnick, in their emphasis on motivation, address the volitional changes in a person and reveal that emotions do accelerate change. They can range from one's fear of death and eternity in hell, hatred of God, gratitude for grace, love for God, to hope of glory. Psychotherapist Diana Fosha says, "core affect, or more precisely, core affective experience, refers to our emotional responses when we do not try to mask, block, distort, or severely mute them."[157] Fosha believed that core affect was the central agent of change and transformation.

> A state of transformation can be achieved through accessing either of two types of core affective experiences: *core emotions* and a *core state. Core emotions*, such as anger, joy sadness, fear, and disgust (i.e., categorical emotions), are in a class by themselves ... *The core state*, a concept introduced and elaborated herein, refers to an altered state of openness and contact, where the individual is deeply in touch with essential aspects of his own experience. The core state is the internal affective holding environment generated by the self.[158]

---

[156] William R. Miller and Stephen Rollnick, *Motivational Interviewing: Preparing People for Change,* 2d ed. (New York: The Guilford Press, 2002), 12.

[157] Diana Fosha, *The Transforming Power of Affect: A Model For Accelerated Change* (New York: Basic Books, 2000), 15.

[158] Ibid., 20.

In commenting on change, Danny Yeung, a physician and clinical counsellor, writes, "We must start from where our patients are and move them along the Stages of Change continuum. We need to be mindful of the question: Where is he/she on the Stages of Change journey?"[159] The study of conversion and change in the literature review challenges evangelicals to ask a similar question concerning those with whom they are sharing the gospel: Where are they in their spiritual journey? How can Christians move them along in the stages of change journey in conversion?

Richard Peace defines the conversion process in terms of changes in insight, turning, and transformation. It is first a change in insight concerning who you are and who God is. It is secondly a turning from sin and the hardness of one's heart to Jesus by repentance and faith. It is thirdly a transformation resulting in forgiveness, discipleship, and a new life. Peace writes, "At the core of the concept of conversion is the idea of turning. On one side of that turning are the conditions that facilitate or enable the turning to take place (insight). On the other side of the turning is the outcome or result of turning (transformation)."[160] Another result in the transformation process with forgiveness, discipleship, and a new life that should be added is a new calling.

Each of these models of change reveals that change is a complicated process and that conversion is a process that moves the convert toward transformation. The practice of pre-discipleship is a way of moving a person along the change journey in conversion.

The models for change and conversion reveal that pre-discipleship can play a role in the conversion process. These psychological and theological models have established that the changes that occur in conversion are seldom dramatic and often gradual and that people come to Christ by different means and at different paces. The fact that it takes time for the majority of people to be converted means that a majority of people need to go through some type of pre-discipleship process before their conversion. Prochaska's model of change called for a preparation

---

[159] Danny Yeung, *Getting to Yes: The ABCs of Changing Problem Behaviors,* March, 2003. Department of Family and Community Medicine, University of Toronto.
[160] Peace, 37.

stage, in which pre-discipleship is ideal since it begins the conversion process toward transformation. Gordon Smith wisely writes,

> We cannot think effectively and biblically about conversion until we take seriously both the possibility of and the call to transformation. This is, properly speaking, the goal of all of the church's life and thus of theological reflection. Conversion therefore is not an end but a beginning; we give it particular attention to encourage the spiritual transformation that is meant to begin.[161]

In conclusion, the analysis of many theological and psychological studies on conversion shows that conversion is more a gradual process than a dramatic single event for the majority of believers. However, many evangelistic methods are based on dramatic conversions. There is a need to allow time for the changes that result in transformation. This means that pre-discipleship, which provides time for change to occur, has a place in the conversion process. Pre-discipleship is one of the many means that God uses to change people in evangelism.

---

[161] Gordon T. Smith, *Beginning Well: Christian Conversion and Authentic Transformation* (Downers Grove, IL: InterVarsity Press, 2001), 19–20.

CHAPTER SEVEN:

PRE-DISCIPLESHIP LEADING TO DISCIPLESHIP

At the heart of the Great Commission is the command to "make disciples." Gene Getz points out, "The church therefore exists to carry out two functions—evangelism (to make disciples) and edification (to teach them)."[162] Yet, in many churches, discipleship has been reduced to a program, a Sunday school class, or an item on a list of things to do. Leroy Eims, in his 1978 book on discipleship, notes that many North American churchgoers know little about discipleship. He writes, "This concept of multiplying disciples has not been as widely accepted as it is today. At one time, in fact not too long ago, relatively few people were doing it. But many more today are returning to that biblical process."[163]

Since Eims' book was published, a significant number of discipleship movements, materials, programs, and conferences have been developed in North American churches. Many pastors and leaders acknowledge the need for discipleship, and yet it is difficult today to find a North American church model that exemplifies biblical discipleship. Today, nearly thirty years after Eims' book, discipleship is still not part of the fabric of most churches.

Many factors have been suggested as the reason why discipleship does not play an important role in churches today. One is that Christians are often too busy with meetings, functions, and even

---

[162] Gene A. Getz, *Sharpening the Focus of the Church* (Chicago: Moody Press, 1981), 22.
[163] Leroy Eims, *The Lost Art of Discipleship Making* (Grand Rapids, MI: Zondervan Publishing House, 1978), 20.

ministry to have time for discipleship. Discipleship author Bill Hull points out, "The modern church is more mired in institutionalism than its first-century counterpart. Whereas the early Christian resisted change because he experienced a vibrant, caring environment, today many resist expansion because it threatens their power base."[164]

Another reason given for discipleship not playing a significant role in the church is the crisis with authority in today's postmodern world. Discipleship programs of the past have always worked in an authoritative structure. However, the postmodern generation does not naturally embrace inherent authorities just because of their position in an established structure. Jimmy Long writes, "Postmodern Xers have no faith in institutions and put little stock in a chain of command. Their respect is earned, not demanded. While not attacking hierarchy directly, they just ignore authority or work around it because as a group they learned to survive in their youth by avoiding conflict."[165]

A third reason why discipleship does not play a predominant role in today's churches may be the pre-discipleship factor. Could it be that one of the reasons why discipleship is rarely practiced is that there is no practice of pre-discipleship leading into discipleship?

This chapter first analyzes the meaning of biblical discipleship to develop a common definition of discipleship. Then it looks at the essence of biblical discipleship with a focus on its characteristics and processes and at how Christians today practice discipleship. Then it concludes by showing the connections between discipleship and pre-discipleship, revealing the significant role pre-discipleship can have in making disciples.

THE MEANING OF BIBLICAL DISCIPLESHIP

It is imperative to define discipleship since many church leaders have misunderstood it, resulting in many inconsistencies in its practice.

---

[164] Bill Hull, *The Disciple-Making Church* (Grand Rapids, MI: Fleming H. Revell, 1994), 91.

[165] Jimmy Long, *Generating Hope: A Strategy for Reaching the Postmodern Generation* (Downers Grove, IL: InterVarsity Press, 1997), 45.

Some church leaders see discipleship as a didactic spiritual relationship while others view it as a program in the church. The understanding of how to practice discipleship ranges from establishing a mentoring relationship to providing a Sunday school class. A biblical definition of discipleship will assist in eliminating common misunderstandings on the subject and improve in the ministry of discipleship in the church.

The word "disciple" came from the Greek word μαθητής, which means "learner," "pupil," or "follower." It is found over 250 times in the New Testament, mostly in the four gospels. According to Kittel, discipleship is more than a cognitive exercise in learning.

> The emphasis is not so much on the incompleteness or even deficiency of education as on the fact that the one thus designated [a disciple] is engaged in learning, that his education consists in the appropriation or adoption of specific knowledge or conduct, and that it proceeds deliberately and according to a set plan. There is thus no μαθητής without a διδάσκαλος. The process involves a corresponding personal relationship.[166]

Although some have suggested that making disciples was not an emphasis of the New Testament church because the word μαθητής is no longer found after Acts 21, the concept is present in the New Testament epistles. Bill Hull explains, "The authors of the Epistles develop replacement words or phrases for *disciple*. Examples include *believer, brother, Christian, faithful, imitators, saints, the called*. Words used to describe function include *model, practice, train, mature,* and *example*. To describe the relationship with the world they used *ambassador, alien,* and *pilgrim*."[167]

What is biblical discipleship? The basic understanding in the New Testament is that all believers are disciples of Christ, followers of Jesus. As mentioned in the previous chapter, young Jewish boys grew

---

[166] Kittel, 416.
[167] Hull, 19.

up wanting to be rabbis, and giving up one's life to pursue God under the study of a rabbi was an accepted behaviour. Believers in the early church were known as the *"followers of this Way"* (Acts 22:4), and "the Way," as Joseph Fitzmyer points out, is "a name for Christianity."[168] Believers in Athens were called *"followers of Paul"* (Acts 17:34), an indication that they thought in terms of being a disciple of a rabbi. The Corinthian believers were divided in their allegiances, an issue Paul addressed. *"My brothers, some from Chloe's household have informed me that there are quarrels among you. What I mean is this: One of you says, 'I follow Paul'; another, 'I follow Apollos'; another, 'I follow Cephas'; still another, 'I follow Christ'"* (1 Corinthians 1:11-12). Paul clarified the concept of being a follower by pointing out that we are following Christ and exhorting the Corinthians to *"follow my example, as I follow the example of Christ"* (1 Corinthians 11:1) Paul used the word "example" in his letter to the Philippians. *"Join with others in following my example, brothers, and take note of those who live according to the pattern we gave you"* (Philippians 3:17). Paul saw himself as the model for following Jesus. He told the Thessalonians, *"We did this, not because we do not have the right to such help, but in order to make ourselves a model for you to follow"* (2 Thessalonians 3:9). The Apostle Peter described Jesus as an example for people to follow: *"To this you were called, because Christ suffered for you, leaving you an example, that you should follow in his steps"* (1 Peter 2:21). Robert Foster summarizes the meaning of discipleship:

> The man or woman who would follow Christ totally must always be a learner, one who is open and teachable. A disciple realizes that he does not have all the answers. This is a crucial area, for we are in great danger if we think we have nothing more to learn in

---

[168] Joseph A. Fitzmyer, *The Acts of the Apostles,* The Anchor Bible (New York: Doubleday, 1998), 735.

our Christian life. A disciple of Jesus Christ is always willing to learn something new from someone else.[169]

THE ESSENCE OF DISCIPLESHIP

The biblical understanding of discipleship provides a basis for reviewing the literature on discipleship to gain an understanding of the essence of discipleship. This essence can be identified by examining both the characteristics of disciples and the processes of discipleship that leaders in the discipleship movement have highlighted as being core to their models. Understanding these characteristics and processes may assist in forming a model of the core essence of pre-discipleship.

Characteristics of Disciples

One of the ways we can understand the essence of discipleship is to study the characteristics of a disciple. To do this, Dawson Trotman, founder of The Navigators, developed a wheel illustration, with Christ in the center and the obedient Christian connected to Christ by two vertical spokes of the word and prayer and two horizontal spokes of witnessing and fellowship. The wheel "shows how Christ should be the center of our lives, that we should live in obedience to him, communicate with him through the Word and prayer, and reach out to others through fellowship and witness."[170] The Navigator model has been influential in the development other models of Christian growth over the years. Others who made important contributions to concepts of discipleship and were in ministry with The Navigators include Richard Foster, Leroy Eims, and Walter Henrichsen.

Foster describes eleven characteristics of a disciple of Jesus Christ. The disciple must 1) be open and teachable, becoming a learner; 2) follow Jesus as Lord; 3) live a life of purity; 4) regularly spend time in devotions and prayer; 5) commit himself or herself to the study and meditation of the word of God; 6) see the importance of being a witness

---

[169] Robert D. Foster, *Essentials of Discipleship* (Colorado Springs, CO: NavPress, 1982), 16.
[170] Eims, 79.

of God and engage in evangelism; 7) be highly involved with church and body life; 8) be involved with Christian fellowship; 9) display servanthood in Christ; 10) enjoy the ministry of giving; and 11) display the fruit of the Spirit.

Foster considers these eleven elements to be "the biblical profile of a disciple." He writes, "Please note that a person who sincerely desires to be a disciple will include these characteristics as part of his or her life, but he or she is not limited to just these eleven. Other biblical characteristics will be part of that person's life as well."[171]

As effective as the Navigator model has been in bringing many towards maturity in Christ, it did not include some important aspects of Christian life. For example, it can be debated whether more spokes would have strengthened the wheel illustration, such as worship, love, accountability, holiness, ministry, service, and giving. On the other hand, it could be argued that these additional spokes are included in the four main Navigator spokes. However, discipleship should never be seen as being this simplistic.

Harold Percy, who identifies six elements of discipleship, proposes a model for understanding discipleship using the analogy of food and exercise. Percy writes, "The food we need to nourish us in our spiritual growth is scripture, worship, and community. Our exercise will be prayer, ministry, and stewardship. If we have only food, our growth will not be healthy; if we have only exercise we will not last. Both food and exercise are required for healthy growth."[172] Percy's food and exercise model covers most of the key aspects of discipleship. However, it reduces discipleship to an individual list of things to do with little emphasis on mentoring relationships and accountability.

In his model of discipleship, Gary Kuhne uses the concept of faithful men who were candidates to be disciples. He argues that although all who profess faith in Christ are candidates for discipleship, not all who claim to be a Christian are faithful. According to Kuhne, the faithful man is a person who hungers for God's word, thirsts for

---

[171] Foster, 14.
[172] Harold Percy, *Following Jesus: First Steps On The Way* (Toronto: Anglican Book Centre, 1993), 8.

holy living, desires a greater knowledge of God, commits to the lordship of Christ, desires to be used by God, and has a love for people. Kuhne stresses that "each of these criteria will only be in seed form in the new Christian. Obviously, as a Christian grows in Christ these characteristics will become deeper and more complete. Yet I believe the seeds of such characteristics are discernible, even in a newer Christian's life."[173] Although Kuhne describes some of the characteristics of a mature disciple, his picture of a disciple seems more of a goal to be obtained in the discipleship journey than the experience in the journey itself. The essence of discipleship, a disciple's love for God and other people, is seen in the characteristics of disciples shown in each area of growth as mentioned in the discipleship models of Trotman, Foster, Percy, and Kuhne.

Process of Discipleship

Another way to understand the essence of discipleship is through a study of the discipleship process. Allan Coppedge, who provides a basic model of discipleship, summarizes the discipleship process as being "divided into three essential principles: life-to-life transference, spiritual disciplines, and accountability."[174] Coppedge defines life transference as occurring "when a person shares wisdom, knowledge, experience, and maturity with another."[175] He points out that life transference occurs when the disciple maker and the disciple spend time together, expend energy with each other, share in a community, and share life together. This life-to-life transference is the same as the mentoring that is promoted today, which Paul Stanley defines as "a relational experience in which one person empowers another by sharing God given resources."[176] David Watson concurs, pointing out that "no man is an island. Our lives are woven together, so that who we are and

---

[173] Gary W. Kuhne, *The Dynamics of Discipleship Training: Being and Producing Spiritual Leaders* (Grand Rapids, MI: Zondervan Publishing House, 1981), 28–29.

[174] Allan Coppedge, *The Biblical Principles Of Discipleship* (Grand Rapids, MI: Francis Asbury Press, 1989), 61.

[175] Ibid.

[176] Paul D. Stanley and J. Robert Clinton, *Connecting: The Mentoring Relationship You Need to Succeed in Live* (Colorado Springs: NavPress, 1992), 38.

what we do always influences other people. The New Testament, therefore, knows nothing of the solitary Christian."[177]

The second principle in the discipleship process is, according to Coppedge, the practice of spiritual disciplines, which he defines as the disciplines of spending time with the word of God, Scripture memorization, fellowship, giving, prayer, fasting, and public worship. Michael Wilkins, who describes these spiritual disciplines as keys to maturity in Christ, points out that "throughout church history, the development of 'spiritual disciplines' has been seen to be a key to spiritual growth."[178]

The third principle of the discipleship process, according to Coppedge, was the principle of accountability. According to Steven Manskar, who believes in what is called covenant discipleship, "the living out of the relationship with Christ through faithful obedience to God and God's commandments" highlights the importance of accountability in discipleship.[179]

> Accountability is how we make sure our discipleship happens. The primary task of Covenant Discipleship is to give disciples the means to prevent and resist the temptation to self-deception. Watching over one another in love helps disciples stand against the trap of believing and living as though they were self-sufficient (having all that is needed, in and of themselves, to be faithful to Christ's call). Mutual accountability prevents us from believing there is no need to "work out [our] own salvation" (Philippians 2:12). Covenant Discipleship also helps people resist the temptation to think they can be disciples when

---

[177] David Watson, *Discipleship* (London: Hodder and Stoughton, 1982), 243.
[178] Michael J. Wilkins, *Following The Master: Discipleship in the Steps of Jesus* (Grand Rapids, MI: Zondervan Publishing House, 1992), 135.
[179] Steven W. Manskar, *Accountable Discipleship: Living In God's Household* (Nashville: Discipleship Resources, 2000), 23.

they feel like it, when it is convenient, when it feels good.[180]

Accountability in discipleship is intentional, personal, and specific. It is intentional in the sense that some people enter into a discipleship covenant to establish responsibilities and boundaries in accountability. Some small groups make group covenants to emphasize members' commitment to each other in the discipleship process. Matt Friedeman affirms that "the group covenant outlines the mutually agreed-upon purpose, goals, and commitments of the group, as well as establishing a format for the weekly meetings."[181]

Although the emphasis and dynamics of the discipleship models developed by Navigators, Percy, Kuhne, and Coppedge vary from model to model, there are commonalities among them. The literature reveals that the following factors are necessary in the discipleship process. One factor is a mentoring relationship involving some aspect of teaching and accountability, since effective discipleship cannot take place apart from nurturing, intimate, and accountable relationships. A second necessary factor is the practice of the spiritual discipline of worship, the study and internalizing of Scripture, prayer, fasting, purity, and fellowship. The third factor of discipleship is the context of ministry. Ministry such as loving, giving, service, and being a witness for Christ are practical expressions of discipleship. Each one of these factors is at the core the essence of discipleship.

THE PRACTICE OF DISCIPLESHIP

One reason that making disciples has been difficult for the local church in the last hundred years is the lack of effective models. The following section will first describe the limitations of trying to adapt models for students in the church. Then it will examine two traditional approaches to the practice of discipleship, the one-on-one approach and the small

---

[180] Ibid., 23–24.

[181] Matt Friedeman, *Accountability Connection* (Wheaton, IL: Victor Books, 1992), 157.

group approach, identifying their impact. Finally, it will examine a third model that could result from combining these two methods.

Student Ministry Model

With discipleship ministry being driven by campus ministry organizations such as Navigators and Campus Crusade for Christ, many of the models of discipleship were originally developed for the student world. However, that zeal for and practice of discipleship did not transfer to the believers in local churches. The methods that para-church organizations have used effectively among students have not fit well in church settings because the audiences are so different. The strategy for discipling students, who have similar backgrounds, is vastly different from that needed in the local church where people vary markedly in age, interest, and background. Similarly, student ministries disciple mostly single people, while the church faces the challenge of discipling those who are married or divorced, those who have young children, or those who are young children or youth themselves. As well, para-church models for discipleship are often inadequate for the church because they fail to lead believers toward engaging in the ordinances and sacraments in the church community.

In an effort to develop a practical model for discipleship in the local church, the church has taken two philosophical approaches resulting in two traditional organizational structures for discipleship in local churches: one-on-one mentoring and small groups. Both approaches have their strengths and limitations.

One-on-One Approach

The one-on-one model ideally involves a mentor and a protégé who, like Paul and Timothy in the New Testament, form an intimate relationship for life. It is the basic structure for intensive discipleship and ideally done on an individual basis. Navigators promoted a concept, which many others have embraced, that by discipling one person a year, and doubling the number of disciples each year, the entire population of the Earth could be discipled in thirty-three years. Messianic Rabbi David Hargis writes, "The discipleship process of

Yeshua is not based on immediate gratification. Yet in one lifetime, through *one-by-one* discipleship, the entire earth can easily be reached with the truth of God's Messiah and God's commandments."[182]

While the one-on-one model has benefits for discipling certain individuals, it has limited effectiveness in a church setting because it may not meet the range of needs in the congregation. The one-on-one discipleship process is also too slow to use in the context of a local church.

The lack of results indicate that this mentoring method has limited effectiveness in reaching the world on the scale supporters have claimed it could. While advocates boast that the world can be won in thirty-three years through one-on-one discipleship, the reality is that this theory has been promoted for more than fifty years and the world is not close to being discipled. A different approach to discipleship in the church seems to be needed.

Small Group Approach

The main model used for small group discipleship is Jesus' three-year relationship with his twelve disciples. Henry Cloud and John Townsend argue that the small group is the best vehicle to bring a disciple to maturity. Writing concerning stagnant Christians, they said, "When people who have been stuck find themselves involved in a small group that is actually doing the things the Bible says to do in that context, life change occurs that has never before occurred."[183] Author and church growth consultant Carl George argues for the effectiveness of small groups, saying he is "convinced that the kind of group that does the best job of 'keeping' people is the mouse-size home-cell group."[184] Bill Hull argues that "effective discipling must take place in a small-group setting. It provides intimacy; a variety of gifts, without an over-whelming atmosphere; and an ideal training vehicle for reproduction. It

---

[182] David Hargis, "The Power of Discipleship"
www.messianic.com/articles/discipleship.htm, accessed October 28, 2008.
[183] Henry Cloud and John Townsend, *Making Small Groups Work* (Grand Rapids, MI: Zondervan, 2003), 29.
[184] Carl F. George, *Prepare Your Church For The Future* (Grand Rapids, MI: Fleming H. Revell, 1992), 74.

teaches well, provides accountability, and can become the launching pad for large group activities."[185]

A leading advocate of the cell-church movement, Joel Comiskey, believes that the cell group is the backbone or center of church ministry. Comiskey argues that the cell church should replace the institutionalized church because it is more effective in discipleship. He writes, "Cell ministry replaces the need for many traditional programs. I like to use the phrase, *the cell-driven church,* because church growth success is primarily measured through infrastructure growth as the church grows from the core to the crowd."[186]

Ralph Neighbour, a strong advocate of cell churches, believes this non-traditional structure creates the community for New Testament discipleship and church life.

> Cell churches are the only way that true community can be experienced by all Christians. It is not a "purest dream" to suggest the church should structure itself around this truth. Rather, it is a return to a life style which has been bastardized by centuries of unbiblical, crusted traditions. The cell group is not just a portion of church life, to be clustered with a dozen other organizations. It is church life; and when it properly exists, all other competing structures are neither needed nor valid.[187]

While the cell-church movement is accurate on many counts in its criticism of the traditional church, it has its own limitations because its solution to the lack of New Testament discipleship is one of infrastructure and organization instead of spirituality. To limit spiritual growth to the confines of a cell group is to put boundaries on the Spirit who moves through a variety of means and vehicles.

---

[185] Hull, 214.
[186] Joel Comiskey, *Cell Church Solutions,* photocopy of manuscript by author, submitted to CCS Publishing, September 13, 2004.
[187] Ralph W. Neighbour Jr., *Where Do We Go From Here?* (Houston: Touch Publications, 1990), 112–113.

Both the one-on-one approach and the small group approach have had some success in creating disciples. Another approach, however, seems to be needed to make disciples of the world. Jim Peterson describes the success of current approaches: "Thirty years of discipleship programs, and we are not discipled."[188] This means that the church needs to begin to understand discipleship in a different way.

Matrix Approach

Since various models of discipleship have strengths and weakness, it is not useful for churches to view the process of discipleship as being an either/or proposition of one-on-one discipleship versus small group discipleship. Scripture itself embraces both and allows for other forms. Rather, discipleship can be better understood in the form of a discipleship matrix that embraces every approach that draws believers to maturity.

The discipleship matrix is not a program, but a philosophy. It recognizes that relationships, programs, environments, cultures, experiences, and church all contribute to a disciple's growth and maturity. The matrix identifies the many types of ministry and relationships in a church that can contribute to developing disciples.

The first component of discipleship in the local church involves everyone in the congregational community helping each other to mature in Christ. The community aspect is a characteristic of the New Testament church. One description of it says that *"all the believers were together"* (Acts 2:44). The early church recognized that members of the body of Christ helped one another in their spiritual journeys and the New Testament emphasizes believers' responsibility towards "one another."

A second component of discipleship in the local church would be gender specific: men helping men and women helping women. This is a useful approach because the most effective discipleship occurs when the leader and group members of a small group, or those in a mentoring relationship, are of the same gender. Gender-specific ministries often

---

[188] Jim Petersen, *Lifestyle Discipleship* (Colorado Springs, CO: NavPress, 1993), 15.

remove barriers created by culture or generation. The Apostle Paul told Timothy, *"Do not rebuke an older man harshly, but exhort him as if he were your father. Treat younger men as brothers, older women as mothers, and younger women as sisters, with absolute purity"* (1 Timothy 5:1-2).

Gender-specific ministries such as Promise Keepers and Women Alive played large roles in the maturing growth of the believer in local churches. Promise Keepers notes that "revival and discipleship are the two elements that became the foundation and focus of Promise Keepers."[189] Women Alive encourages women to "allow the life of Christ to affect every area of their lives and impact the world around them."[190] Churches must not ignore gender-specific ministries because these ministries play a significant role in discipleship today.

A third component of discipleship in the local church happens in cell groups, the place in which he strongest and most intense relationships are formed and care is practiced. Carl George writes, "Primary nurturative care-mutual care of peers encouraging and serving one another requires a cell-level context."[191] The caring relationships that develop in cell groups naturally evolve over time into learning relationships with one another. The first church in Jerusalem not only met in the temple courts, but members met in cells in their homes. *"Every day they continued to meet together in the temple courts. They broke bread in their homes and ate together with glad and sincere hearts, praising God and enjoying the favor of all the people"* (Acts 2:46-47). Cells can be established to meet a variety of needs such as prayer, Bible study, and outreach. Ideally, each cell should function on all levels of ministry, but practically speaking, many cells have their own signature of ministry. All cells, though, should function in the area of caring.

A fourth component of discipleship in the local church is one-on-one relationships. One component of discipleship growth involves

---

[189] Promise Keepers, "The History of Promise Keepers," http://www.promisekeepers.org//about/pkhistory, accessed February 18, 2005.

[190] Women Alive, "About Us," http://www.womenalive.org/aboutus.php, February 18, 2005.

[191] Carl F. George, *Prepare Your Church For The Future*, 126–129.

sharing information with others as one continues to learn through intellectual, emotional, social, and accountable relationships. Within cell groups, a variety of individual relationships are established and they result in one of three kinds of discipleship occurring: passive, occasional, or intensive. Passive discipleship occurs between two individuals when one learns and grows from the other, or vice versa, without any active plan to connect individually. Occasional discipleship happens when individuals meet from time to time to help each other grow in Christ. Intensive discipleship occurs when two individuals meet together for discipleship on a regular basis. All of these discipleship connections mostly in the form of mentor-protégé relationships. Leroy Eims writes, "A ministry of multiplication does not come from an attempt to mass produce disciples. There must be individual, personal time with each person with whom you are working and whom you are training."[192] Paul often encouraged Timothy to carry on these relationships in the local church. *"And the things you have heard me say in the presence of many witnesses entrust to reliable men who will also be qualified to teach others"* (2 Timothy 2:2).

The discipleship matrix recognizes that the church that makes disciples must establish an environment for spiritual growth through its community, men's and women's groups, cell groups, and individual relationships. It must practice a philosophy that sees all ministries as part of the disciple-making process. The discipleship matrix is also consistent with pedagogical systems of adult learning, which will be discussed in the following chapter.

In conclusion, the literature on discipleship indicates that disciples of Christ are learners and followers of Jesus who are always willing to obey. The disciple is open and teachable. Discipleship engages believers in mentoring relationships that involve accountability. It also involves spiritual disciplines includes worship, prayer, and study of the word, often in the context of ministry. It can be and is best understood in its practice in a matrix of approaches embracing the church community, gender-specific ministry, cell groups, and one-on-one relationships.

---

[192] Eims, 102.

CONNECTION BETWEEN DISCIPLESHIP AND PRE-DISCIPLESHIP

The previous review of the elements of discipleship and on approaches to making disciples reveals that there is a significant role for pre-discipleship as preparation for discipleship. It also reveals where connections exist between pre-discipleship and making disciples and why the church can implement pre-discipleship as part of discipleship development.

One connection between pre-discipleship and discipleship can be seen in characteristics shared by pre-disciples and disciples. Both are followers of Christ; disciples are followers of Christ who learn from Him, while pre-disciples are learners who seek to follow Him. The essence, the characteristics and processes, that makes a disciple parallels the essence that makes a pre-disciple. Although pre-disciples do not have the fully matured character of disciples, they have the potential to develop the characteristics of a disciple. Kuhne's description of "faithful men" describes the characteristics of a mature disciple, but he affirms that the characteristics of a young disciple are "in seed form in the new Christian."[193] Although a seeker may have a hunger for God and his word and desire to live a holy life, it is only in the seed form of a magnificent characteristic of something beautiful when matured.

The factors that are necessary in making disciples are similar to important aspects of pre-discipleship processes. The spiritual disciplines of studying the Scripture and of worship, and the desire for the discipline of holiness, are part of pre-discipleship. The ministry of love, giving, and service could all be vital aspects in pre-discipleship. Sometimes seekers are engaged in a voluntary activity as a humanitarian service to the community. However, as they begin to discover God, they begin to discover his purpose through humanitarian activities and thus discover his ministry. While seekers may not experience these factors as deeply as a believer might, the overall experience helps move the unbeliever along the conversion process.

---

[193] Kuhne, 29.

From a methodological perspective, pre-discipleship training could readily be conducted in most churches because, like disciple-making, it functions best in mentoring and accountability relationships. As well, pre-discipleship can be carried out on a variety of levels: the community level, at a cell level, or on an individual level. The mentoring relationship that is so effective for Christians can also be used with those who are not yet believers. Spiritual disciplines are part of the process of pre-discipleship. The accountability and the ministry of love, giving, and service could all be vital aspects of pre-discipleship.

As well, pre-discipleship can help the churches fulfill the mandate of the Great Commission to make disciples, because it leads churches into the kind of relationships in which they are making disciples. Walter Henrichsen writes, "Being a disciple begins with a proper relationship to Jesus Christ and having on your heart what is on His. Making disciples begins with evangelism."[194] As shown earlier, pre-discipleship is an excellent way to accomplish evangelism because in the process, Jesus is introduced to unbelievers through a search in the Scriptures. Once again, pre-discipleship makes discipleship a priority in evangelism.

In conclusion, the analysis of discipleship reveals that its practice, in many ways, gives reflection to pre-discipleship. The investigation of the essence of and approaches to discipleship provides insight on the essence and approaches of pre-discipleship. As the discipleship matrix reveals insight on the variety of ways Christians grow in Christ, a pre-discipleship matrix can also reflect the many ways a seeker comes to Christ. The call to make disciples shows that there is a place for pre-discipleship, a process in evangelism that resonates with the process of conversion leading into discipleship.

---

[194] Walter A. Henrichsen, *Disciples Are Made Not Born* (Wheaton, IL: Victor Books, 1994), 52.

CHAPTER EIGHT:

PRE-DISCIPLESHIP AND CHRISTIAN ADULT EDUCATION

Since pre-discipleship is a form of adult education, a study into adult education is beneficial in providing an understanding of how seekers can best learn in a pre-discipleship process. This chapter will examine whether pre-discipleship has a place in adult religious education and seek to identify effective approaches to the practice of pre-discipleship. To do so, it will look at the history of Christian education, theories of learning, principles of adult religious education, goals of religious education, and the practice of adult Christian education, and how they relate to the practice of pre-discipleship. The chapter answers the question: How can the educational process of pre-discipleship best be conducted to enhance proper conversion and discipleship?

The author acknowledges that there are overlaps in the discussions of the principles, goals, and methods in Christian education. In this focus on Christian education, we must ask the following questions: What are the issues in Christian adult education? Where is Christian education heading? And how can we best practice Christian education?"

THE HISTORY OF CHRISTIAN EDUCATION

Christian education began early in church history, and evidence reveals that the church has historically used education to teach seekers about the Christian faith. This is significant because it means that pre-discipleship is not a recent concept; it has roots in the New Testament church and a legitimate place in churches' Christian education programs today. To prepare adult seekers, the early church used the catechumenate to systematically instruct them on the biblical, theological, and doctrinal aspects of the faith as a means of integrating converts into the church. Leon McKenzie and Michael Harton describe the comprehensive nature of the catechumenate:

> The church's encouragement of lifelong learning is evidenced in the model for learning called the catechumenate. Very early in Christian history an initiatory process for converts to Christianity was assimilated from the pagan mystery religions and Essenian practices. Those who wished to enter the Christian community were required to live in the community for an extended period of time. During this time the catechumen was to learn the ways of the community. At the end of a prescribed time period, a decision was made by leaders of the community (on the basis of the catechumen's acceptance of Christian ways) to permit or forbid further entrance into fellowship. In carefully graded steps the catechumen became incorporated into the community. Biblical knowledge was revealed to the catechumen; he was instructed in moral, social, and liturgical practices. Even after he was admitted into full fellowship through baptism, the new Christian was expected to continue his study of the Scriptures and comment-aries on the Scriptures.[195]

The process was not rushed. Harold Burgess notes that "the period of preparation for the catechumen to become a full communicant

---

[195] Leon McKenzie and R. Michael Harton, *The Religious Education of Adults* (Macon, GA: Smyth & Helwys Publishing Inc., 2002), 32–33.

member was about three years."[196] The church used the catechumenate to conduct adult education during its first four centuries, a period that produced educators such as Clement of Alexandria, Origen, Cyril of Jerusalem, Chrysostom, and Augustine, and education was highly influenced by the Jewish and Greco-Roman cultures.

> Early Christian thought on education was strongly affected by the cultural assumptions of the Jewish and Greco-Roman worlds; these worlds were not always in concordance. Jewish education was thoroughly religious in the explicit sense of the term. Scribes learned to read and write in order to prepare themselves for lifetimes of serious study of the Torah, Mishnah, and Talmud. All education was ordinated directly to theological and explicitly religious themes. Greco-Roman education, on the other hand, was broadly humanistic and explicitly religious values were not taught. Mythology was not studied as religious doctrine but for literary purposes. The study of art, rhetoric, music, philosophy, and literature was an end in itself. This difference in orientation toward education was argued thoroughly by fathers of the early church.[197]

Then during the fifth to fifteenth centuries, Christian education changed from its focus on teaching seekers to training for monks and others who would serve the church, and so the benefits of the catechumenate were lost. The "catechumenal instruction prior to baptism of adult converts was reduced to a ceremonial ritual enacted on behalf of infants at their baptism."[198] Christian education changed during those centuries because of the influence of a range of scholars. In the sixth

---

[196] Harold W. Burgess, *Models of Religious Education* (Nappanee, IN: Evangel Publishing House, 2001), 35–36.
[197] Mckenzie and Harton, 35–36.
[198] Michael J. Anthony ed., *Introducing Christian Education: Foundations for the Twenty-first Century* (Grand Rapids, MI: Baker Academic, 2001), 20.

century, Gregory the Great saw secular learning as unnecessary for Christians, while from the eleventh to thirteenth centuries, Anselm, Peter Abelard, Peter Lombard, and Thomas Aquinas, combined religious and secular education, philosophy, and theology to benefit the church and the community. Adult Christian education during the Middle Ages evolved to the point where seekers likely had difficulty learning about the faith, and teaching on the faith was restricted mainly to members of monastic communities and to the nobility.

As Western Europe began to radically change in the sixteenth century, a thirst for knowledge and education grew. Growing nationalism meant that people were less willing to submit to a distant pope, while an increased interest in ancient Greek and Roman art and literature fuelled the flames of the Renaissance. Those changes, along with anger over the corruption in the church and disagreements over church leadership and doctrine, led to the Reformation. This period saw a growth in public education, a development of catechisms for teaching converts to the Christian faith, and an increasing interest in studying the Bible with respect to its authority in faith and practice. Many of the Reformers embraced the role of education, resulting in education being made more widely available. It was said that Martin Luther believed "the right kind of schools ... would not only prepare individuals for the tasks of industry and government, but they would accomplish the great goal of teaching every Christian to read the Bible."[199] During the Reformation, other influential educators such as Calvin, Zwingli, and John Knox among the Protestants and Ignatius of Loyola among the Catholics contributed to the renewed interest in learning through their examinations of Scripture and theological teaching.

The seventeenth through nineteenth centuries ushered in the years of the Enlightenment, when individualism, pietism, revivalism, and industrialization had significant impact on the world and Christian education. The pursuit of knowledge was widely embraced and the desire for the knowledge of God was common. In this era, educators such as Philipp Jacob Spener, a German Pietist, August Herman Francke, a student of Spener, and Nikolaus Ludwig Zinzendorf, the

---

[199] Burgess, 51.

founder of the Moravians, helped revitalize catechetical instruction so that it could focus on a genuine spiritual experience with God and not just the memorization of a creed.[200]

John Wesley, founder of the Methodist movement, was influenced by the Moravians in his views on education. He helped establish schools for children for spiritual instruction and was one of the first religious leaders to establish a Sunday school as part of his ministry. He saw the connection between evangelism and education: "For Wesley, education was not secondary to evangelism, it was bound together with it. Methodist preachers were charged to 'diligently and earnestly instruct the children' and to make a place for them to grow within the Methodist societal structure."[201]

During the twentieth century, Christian education became more institutionalized. When the role of religious instruction in public education diminished, Christian education for children began moving from the public school arena into the religious school arena. Religious training institutions were also established for adults: "The missions' movement of the late 1800s encouraged the development of Bible institutes and colleges for training young adults to evangelize and disciple others in the faith."[202] Most Christian educational programs ended up specializing in training Christians to live out their faith in the world. In the last century, the growing emphasis on adult education resulted in the growth of adult religious education programs. In spite of that change, little, if any, pre-discipleship is now taught as a part of adult Christian education.

In summary, pre-discipleship was widely practiced throughout church history, beginning with the catechumenate in the early church as a means of integrating converts into the church. Although it was rarely practiced during the Middle Ages, catechisms were written again during the Reformation to teach converts the Christian faith. During the Enlightenment, education in the church among the Moravians and Wesleyans was an integral aspect of evangelism. The history of

---

[200] Anthony, 22.
[201] Burgess, 61–62.
[202] Anthony, 24.

religious education in the church supports the practice of pre-discipleship, even though it has been forgotten in the education of today.

THE THEORIES OF LEARNING

There are five major theories that have influenced adult learning: behaviourist orientation, cognitive orientation, humanist orientation, social learning orientation, and constructivism. Our purpose is to understand how adults gain knowledge and to make determinations that will assist in understanding pre-discipleship from an educational perspective.

The behaviourist theory of learning regards the learning process as a change in behaviour and describes the purpose of education as being to produce behavioural change in a desired direction. The method focuses on measuring aspects of human behaviour in the context of stimuli and responses. Recognized Behaviourism theorists such as Edwin Ray Guthrie, Clark Leonard Hull, Ivan Pavlov, B. F. Skinner, Edward Thorndike, Edward Chace Tolman, and John Watson, believed that behaviour is connected to positive or negative external reinforcements. Skinner understood personality as a "repertoire of behaviour imported by an organized set of contingencies."[203] In other words, people learn and from their characters as a result of their environment. The behaviourist orientation can assist in establishing behavioural objectives, skill development, and training in adult learning and has relevance in terms of setting behavioural goals in pre-discipleship.

In contrast, the cognitive orientation to learning regards learning as an internal mental process that involves insight, data processing, memory, and perception. Its purpose of education is to develop the capacity and skills to learn better. Leaders of the cognitivist camp like David Ausubel, Jerome Bruner, Robert Gagné, Kurt Koffka, Wolfgang Köhler, Kurt Lewin, and Jean Piaget believed that perception, insight,

---

[203] B.F. Skinner, *About Behaviorism* (New York: Knopf, 1974), 149.

and meaning are keys to learning. Cognitivists would say that the mind is always learning and actively processing information. They believe that "the human mind is not simply a passive exchange-terminal system where the stimuli arrive and the appropriate response leaves. Rather, the thinking person interprets sensations and gives meaning to the events that impinge upon his consciousness."[204] This learning theory encourages adults to learn how to recognize their ability to process and retrieve information as they age. This orientation has significance to addressing the internal mental structure of a seeker in pre-discipleship.

The humanist orientation developed by Abraham Maslow and Carl Rogers regards the learning process as a personal act to fulfill potential, and the purpose of education as a means to become self-actualized and autonomous. Rogers identified the following characteristics of learning:

1. *Personal involvement:* the affective and cognitive aspects of a person should be involved in the learning event.

2. *Self-initiated:* a sense of discovery must come from within.

3. *Pervasive:* the learning makes a difference in the behavior, the attitudes, perhaps even the personality of the learner.

4. *Evaluated by the learner:* the learner can best determine whether the experience is meeting a need.

5. *Essence is meaning:* when experiential learning takes place, its meaning to the learner becomes incorporated into the total experience.[205]

This humanistic orientation leads to a clearer understanding of andragogy, the art and science of helping adults learn, and of models of

---

[204] P. Grippin and S. Peters, *Learning Theory and Learning Outcomes: The Connection,* (Lanham, MD: University Press of America, 1984), 76.
[205] Carl R. Rogers, *Freedom to Learn for the 80s,* (Columbus, OH: Charles E. Merrill, 1983), 20.

self-directed learning in the adult learner. A case can be made that the seeker in the pre-discipleship process is a self-directed learner.

The social learning orientation sees the learning process as an interaction with and observation of others in a social context. Proponents of this theory are Albert Bandura and Julian Rotter, who see the purpose of education as being to model new roles and behaviour for the learner. Bandura believed that learning from observation is cognitive and vicarious. He writes, "Virtually all learning phenomena resulting from direct experiences can occur on a vicarious basis through observation of other people's behavior and its consequences for the observer."[206] This learning theory manifests itself in social roles and mentoring in adult learning when learners observe their leader's interactions in a social context. Social learning is evident in the case of a seeker of faith who is observing and learning from Christians' behaviour, an important aspect of the pre-discipleship process.

Constuctivism sees the learning process as a construction of meaning from experience. The leading constructivists, Jean Piaget, P.C. Candy, John Dewey, Jean Lave, B. Rogoff, Ernst von Glaserfeld, and Lev Vygotsky, believed the purpose of education was for learners to construct new knowledge from their experiences. "Meaning is made by the individual and is dependent on the individual's previous and current knowledge structure. Learning is thus an internal cognitive activity."[207] The constructivist theory does not espouse a particular pedagogy, but allows students to learn and come up with their own understanding depending upon their background and experiences. The constructivist model explains why students can come to their own conclusions through the process of pre-discipleship.

In summary, these five major theories of learning all have significance in identifying qualities that need to be in pre-discipleship programs. The behaviourist orientation addresses the need for a behavioural goal. In theological terms, this behavioural goal should be considered as "repentance." The cognitive orientation addresses the

---

[206] Albert Bandura, *Modeling Theory,"* in *Learning Systems, Models, and Theories,* W. S. Sahakian ed., 2nd ed. (Chicago: Rand McNally, 1976), 392.
[207] Sharan B. Merriam and Rosemary S. Caffarella, *Learning in Adulthood: A Comprehensive Guide,* 2d ed. (San Francisco, CA: Jossey-Bass, 1999), 262.

need for pre-discipleship to contain elements that appeal to the intellect and enable the seeker to gain insight, information, and perceptions about Christianity. The humanist orientation identifies the importance of respecting the seeker in the pre-discipleship process. The rise of andragogy and self-directed learning allows the pre-discipleship process to be less dependent on the teacher. The social learning orientation speaks to the need of modeling and of mentorship in pre-discipleship. One-on-one settings and group settings provide healthy environments for the interaction that enable seekers to learn about Christ. The constructivist theory indicates that pre-discipleship can be experienced in a variety of ways; allowing for this enables seekers to come to their own conclusions about Christ. Each one of these learning theories contributes to understanding how adults learn and to a pedagogical understanding of pre-discipleship.

THE PRINCIPLES OF ADULT RELIGIOUS EDUCATION

Since this book is focusing on educating the adult seeker in the basics of Christianity, it is important to understand how adults learn best by examining the principles of effective adult education. What are the issues in adult education and how do they apply to pre-discipleship? Nancy Foltz, a leading authority on adult learning, has identified ten basic principles concerning the adult learner.[208]

The first three principles relate to the physical health of the adult learners and how it affects their ability to respond appropriately during learning. First, the capacity to learn does not necessarily decline with age, but natural losses in hearing and sight can affect the learning process. Second, the loss of hearing can contribute to other problems, such as a loss of accuracy of information received, a loss of self-confidence and security, a change in interpersonal relations, and adjustments to using supportive devices. Third, the accuracy of response is not necessarily affected by age, but the speed of response is. These three principles indicate that some adults do have physical limit-

---

[208] Nancy T. Foltz ed., *Handbook of Adult Religious Education* (Birmingham, AL: Religious Education Press, 1986), 45–53.

ations that affect their ability to learn and that they all learn at different paces. Foltz pointed out that "rushing the adult learner can be nonproductive. Allowing time for to complete their learning increases their sense of confidence. Always rushing and moving right along may not result in quality thinking and work."[209] Foltz's comment here concerning process supports the concept of providing time in evangelistic outreach that some people need for coming to faith, something that the pre-discipleship process does.

According to Foltz, the fourth principle concerning adult learners is that they learn best when they are not under stress. Foltz writes, "When unemployment and marriage conflicts arise adults experience stress and need additional supports to sustain emotional and psychological strength."[210] This principle means that pre-discipleship should not be practiced without first addressing the basic needs of the adult learner. When physical needs of food, shelter, clothing, and health and emotional needs like healthy relationships are not met, this can distract from learning. This means that in outreach, it is best to meet the basic needs of an individual before engaging in any form of pre-discipleship.

The fifth principle concerning the adult learner is that time is valuable to them; they enter learning environments on a voluntary basis and are very aware of the factors of time. Patricia Cross and A. Zusman identify a "lack of time" as the number one barrier to participation in learning. Cross writes, "The major barriers of lack of time and, to a lesser extent, costs are actually complex barriers in which the message is that participation in educational activities is not as high in priority as other things that adults might wish to do or to spend their money on at this stage in their lives."[211] Adults have no interest in wasting time and therefore any pre-discipleship process must be mindful of this. The time factor is critical in the development of pre-discipleship materials. Materials that take three months to digest will be more appealing than materials that take a year to digest. Materials that need only seven

---

[209] Ibid., 47.
[210] Ibid.
[211] K. Patricia Cross, *Adults as Learners: Increasing Participation and Facilitating Learning,* (San Francisco, CA: Jossey-Bass Publishers, 1981), 146.

weeks to complete will be even more appealing than materials that require a commitment of three months.

The sixth principle is that the adult learner is problem-centered rather than subject-centered, as indicated by the sales of millions of "how-to" books, which identify a problem and offer a series of steps for reaching a solution. Adults are motivated to learn in order to resolve problems, whether the problem is fixing a marriage, house, or a problem in their life. Foltz writes, "Effective adult religious education brings together the needs of the adults with creative ways to discuss and resolve those needs."[212] In light of this principle, pre-discipleship is more appealing to seekers when it addresses their felt needs and answers their questions, such as "How can I know for sure that God exists?" "How can I know God?" "How can I know for sure that the Bible is the word of God?" "How can I understand the Bible?" "How can I be sure about who Jesus is?" "How can I find true love?" and "How can I deal with my sin?"

The seventh principle is that adult learners are self-directed. Self-directed learning is self-planned and done at the learners' pace and in their style of learning. Anne Poonwassie, a practitioner in adult education, writes, "It has become clear that learning takes place anywhere and at any time, far beyond adults' planned and organized educational experiences, and the development of self-directed learning has become a priority and 'a prerequisite for living in this new world.'"[213] Self-directed learners are naturally motivated. Author Gary Dickinson writes, "Intrinsic sources of motivation derive from within the individual and include curiosity, the desire to master a subject, need for achievement, and striving for knowledge for its own sake."[214] Patricia Cross states, "the explosion of knowledge means that almost all professionals are self-directed learners; but most are also spending increasing amounts of time in a wide variety of organized learning

---

[212] Foltz, 50.

[213] Anne Poonwassie, "Facilitating Adult Education: A Practitioner's Perspective," eds. Deo H. Poonwassie and Anne Poonwassie, *Fundamentals of Adult Education* (Toronto, ON: Thompson Educational Publishing, Inc., 2001), 152.

[214] Gary Dickinson, *Teaching Adults: A Handbook for Instructors,* (Toronto, ON: New Press, 1973), 40.

activities."[215] This principle has significant implications for pre-discipleship in that those engaged in the practice are seekers motivated to learn about Christianity and can engage in pre-discipleship through self-study at their own pace.

The eighth principle of adult learning is that adult learners are interested in immediate application of learning. Author Alan Knox writes, "Usually participants want to apply or use what they learn in order to strengthen their performance in one or more adult life roles."[216] This principle means that pre-discipleship must be relevant and applicable to the seeker. Information that has no bearing upon a seeker's life is of little value.

The ninth principle concerning the adult learner is that some adult learners are goal-oriented, some learning-oriented, and others activity-oriented. Different adults have different motives for learning because of differences in their brains and the way they process information. Marlene LeFever identifies four styles of learners: imaginative learners, analytic learners, common sense learners, and dynamic learners. An understanding of how different people learn can be used to inform the pre-discipleship process:

> Not only is each person most comfortable in a particular style, but each style benefits the whole learning process. Imaginative learners help answer the question, "Why do I need this?" They enjoy talking and sharing their life experiences. Without them, other students may not grasp the personal value of what will be taught. Analytic learners help answer the question, "What does the Bible say about my need?" They enjoy learning new facts and concepts. Without them, other students may not build an intellectual understanding of the Bible. Common sense learners help answer the question, "How does

---

[215] Cross, 30.

[216] Alan B. Knox, *Helping Adults Learn* (San Francisco, CA: Jossey-Bass Publishers, 1990), 188.

what the Bible teaches actually work?" They enjoy experimenting. Without them, other students may not practice how biblical values work today. Dynamic learners help answer the question, "Now, how will I use what I have learned?" They enjoy finding creative ways to put faith into action. Without them, other students may not discover a "practical" faith.[217]

Since adults tend to learn in different ways, pre-discipleship programs need to be fluid in adapting to the learning processes of the seekers. This means that, while the pre-discipleship content can remain the same, its presentation must be adjusted to the learning styles of the seekers. Creativity in presentation is important in pre-discipleship. LeFever comments, "Christians are not always viewed as creative people, either by ourselves or the secular world. We tend to limit ourselves and what we are able to do with the talents and gifts God has given."[218]

LeFever also encourages teachers to learn how the creative process works. She writes, "Knowing what happens in these steps can keep us from making mistakes that limit our creativity or becoming frustrated because things aren't happening the way we think they should, as we sweat and strain toward our goal. The steps in the process are: (1) Preparation, (2) Incubation, (3) Illumination, (4) Elaboration, and (5) Verification."[219] The process of pre-discipleship can best be presented in a creative manner adapted to the learning style of each seeker. For example, the pre-discipleship process with an analytic learner will focus more on data and facts, while with a dynamic learner it will have more emphasis on application. Pre-discipleship cannot be rigid in presentation, but must be fluid, adapting to the adult seekers' learning styles and what motivates them.

---

[217] Marlene D. LeFever, *Learning Styles: Reaching Everyone God Gave You To Teach* (Paris, ON: David C. Cook Publishing Co., 1995), 16.
[218] Marlene D. LeFever, *Creative Teaching Methods* (Weston, ON: David C. Cook Publishing Co., 1985), 21.
[219] Ibid., 25.

The tenth principle of the adult learner is that the adult can construct an expanded perception of the world. Adults who grasp spiritual truths can begin to understand the relevancy of those truths to the world and their global ramifications. This principle of learning may have more significance to the truths of missions than for the seeker in pre-discipleship.

In summary, nine out of Nancy Foltz's ten principles of the adult learner have relevance to pre-discipleship because they provide valuable insight on how pre-discipleship needs to be practiced in the world. Understanding the principles related to physical limitations, stress, time, problem solving, self-direction, immediate application, motivation, and global perspectives is important for effective adult learning and pre-discipleship.

THE GOALS IN CHRISTIAN EDUCATION

The section on the history of Christian education has established that educating adults in the basics of Christianity has historical precedent, while the last two sections identified pedagogical support for pre-discipleship in theories of learning and principles of adult religious education. We now examine valid goals for Christian education and how they apply to pre-discipleship, because goals influence the development of programs.

Jack Seymour identifies four primary themes in Christian education, which could be used to set direction and goals: "(1) the mission of the church in the world, (2) the role of the faith community, (3) the understanding of the person, and (4) the place of instruction."[220] Seymour also developed the four themes into four approaches to Christian education: transformation, faith community, spiritual growth, and religious instruction.

Seymour identifies one goal in Christian education as social transformation, a process involving radical change and crisis, as well as spiritual transformation, which begins at conversion. Daniel Schipani

---

[220] Jack L. Seymour, ed., *Mapping Christian Education: Approaches to Congregational Learning* (Nashville: Abingdon Press, 1997), 18–19.

writes that the "Christian faith must play a role in the transformation of society and culture."[221] If the goal of Christian education is social transformation, then one way this can be achieved is through pre-discipleship, which ultimately leads people to Jesus so that their lives will be transformed through Christ.

A second goal in Christian education is building community. Christian education was never meant to be solely an individual pursuit, but people are to learn in the context of community.

> Community, as a goal for religious education, means three things: (1) a normative ideal; (2) reflection and support; and (3) a dialectic process. First, as a normative ideal, the community approach to education links both personal and communal development ... Second, reflection and support takes place through the conversations of the groups ... Third, viewing the conversation about people's lives collectively is a dialectic process that empowers people to reengage in community building.[222]

As demonstrated in the previous chapter, pre-discipleship education meets this goal of building community. It is not solely about a person's journey in gathering information about the Christian faith, but also about engaging in supportive relationships in Christian community.

A third goal in Christian education is spiritual growth of both the community and the individual in the community.

> Growth became the metaphor for development because it seemed to be the only alternative for an endpoint that thwarts human creativity. But the metaphor of growth, taken from biology and mathematics, is too primitive for describing personal

---

[221] Ibid., 26.
[222] Ibid., 48–49.

> development. A person develops in relation to
> wholeness: The deeper the inwardness, the more
> integral the communion of persons. Of course,
> aspects of that development can be described as
> growth, but other aspects could be called *shrinking* or
> *simplification.* A Christian view of development has
> no *endpoint* (what Christianity calls an idol) but it
> moves toward a definite end: the communion of
> all.[223]

Although those who believe that an unbeliever is spiritually dead
might argue that there is no spiritual growth within pre-discipleship, a
case can be made that there is movement within a pre-disciple on the
spiritual journey toward Christ.

A fourth goal in Christian education is religious instruction.
Elizabeth Caldwell believes that religious instruction is homemaking,
"a connective, creative act of the human imagination and a primary
activity of Spirit. It is the creation of forms and patterns which cultivate
and shelter life itself."[224]

> What is missing in such congregations is an ethos of
> a faithful learning community that empowers by its
> planning for faithful learning across the ages. Or in
> other words, making a home as a learning and
> growing community of Christians has been forgotten
> or abandoned. The church as a place of homemaking
> with a great room of people, using content and
> methods that integrate worship, education, mission,
> stewardship, and community is here never consid-
> ered.[225]

---

[223] Ibid., 69–70.
[224] Ibid., 77.
[225] Ibid., 78.

Caldwell observed that in religious education, the goals for adults in many congregations are different from those for children and youth, when they should be the same. Christian education should aim to transform lives, build the community, encourage spiritual growth, and develop an environment for religious instruction.

As this section shows, the goals of Christian education, which lead to healthy change, growth, and learning on the spiritual journey in the context of community, can be realized through pre-discipleship. It also provides additional support for the practice of pre-discipleship for seekers in adult Christian education.

THE PRACTICE OF ADULT CHRISTIAN EDUCATION

The theories of learning and the principles of adult education previously discussed provide insight on how adults can gain knowledge regarding the Christian faith and principles to guide the process. We now shift to the practical side of adult education and discuss ways to implement these theories and principles. We will examine the literature to identify how pre-discipleship can best be practiced. Some methods commonly used for adult education, such as classes, workshops, seminars, and conferences, have been the standard means of educating adults. However, other factors are useful in adult Christian education. Many scholars are qualified to provide practical insights on adult Christian education, but this section examines the work of two key authors. The first is Jane Vella, a leading expert on adult education, and the other is Leonard Sweet, a leading authority on teaching the postmodern adult.

Jane Vella, who believes that the best means of educating adults is through dialogue, identifies twelve principles for effective adult learning, principles that have relevance for pre-discipleship.

> One basic assumption in all this is that adult learning
> is best achieved in dialogue. *Dia* means "between,"
> *logos* means "word." Hence, *dia* + *logue* = "the word
> between us." The approach to adult learning based on
> these principles holds that adults have enough life

134

experience to be in dialogue with any teacher about any subject and will learn new knowledge, attitudes, or skills best in relation to that life experience. Danah Zohar calls dialogue a quantum process, the means of doing quantum thinking. In this approach to adult learning all twelve principles and practices are ways to begin, maintain, and nurture the dialogue:

- *Need assessment:* participation of the learners in naming what is to be learned.
- *Safety* in the environment and the process. We create a context for learning. That context can be made safe.
- *Sound relationships* between teacher and learner and among learners.
- *Sequence* of content and *reinforcement.*
- *Praxis:* action with reflection or learning by doing.
- *Respect for learners as decision makers.*
- *Ideas, feelings, and actions:* cognitive, affective, and psychomotor aspects of learning.
- *Immediacy* of the learning.
- *Clear roles and role development.*
- *Teamwork* and the use of small groups.
- *Engagement* of learners in what they are learning.
- *Accountability:* how do they know they know![226]

Engagement in dialogue is ideal in the pre-discipleship process. While not all adults learn through dialogue, and some may be self-directed learners, the majority of adult learners benefit from dialogue

---

[226] Jane Vella, *Learning to Listen, Learning to Teach: The Power of Dialogue in Educating Adults* (San Francisco, CA: Jossey-Bass, 2002), 3–4.

education. Vella pointed out that "this model of dialogue education assumes that human beings come to learning with some appetite, and that they can and will make intelligent choices."[227] Dialogue is the best means of practicing pre-discipleship. Those who participate in pre-discipleship are motivated to learn about God and his truths.

Dialogue appeals to post-modern adults, who learn differently than people raised under the influence of cognitive-oriented models of modernity, because it allows them to discuss issues openly and safely. Leonard Sweet writes, "Post-moderns don't want to 'study under' any authority figure; they want to study the authority figure. They don't need 'authorities' to help them gain information. But ironically, they need 'authorities' more than ever before to mentor them in how to use, perform, and model the information."[228]

Sweet suggests that a practical means of educating postmodern adults is a model he calls EPIC, standing for experiential, participatory, interactive, and communal.[229] The theories of learning and the principles of adult Christian education can be summed up in EPIC, which is consistent with the orientations of the behaviourists, humanists, social learners, and constructivists. EPIC also sets the context in which Vella's use of dialogue in adult education can be applied.

The use of dialogue in the context of experience, participation, interaction, and community are practical means of pre-discipleship. Some seekers need to experience God before making a commitment to Him. Others need to get involved in dialoguing about God in the pre-discipleship process in an interactive community. The practice of adult education in respect to Vella's dialogue and Sweet's EPIC are significant in pre-discipleship.

---

[227] Jane Vella, *Dialogue Education at Work* (San Francisco: Jossey-Bass, 2004), 5.

[228] Leonard Sweet, *Soul Tsunami: Sink or Swim in New Millennium Culture* (Grand Rapids, MI: Zondervan Publishing House, 1999), 187.

[229] Ibid., 215.

SUMMARY OF PRE-DISCIPLESHIP AND ADULT EDUCATION

In summary, this pedagogical study is significant to pre-discipleship in a number of ways. The history of Christian education supports the use of pre-discipleship in the church, showing that it was practiced throughout church history, especially in the early church and during the Enlightenment. The focus on the theories of learning and the principles of adult religious education affirmed that pre-discipleship is a sound pedagogical approach to teaching Christianity. The goals of religious education confirm the need for transformation, spiritual growth, and learning in the context of Christian community, which are applicable to pre-discipleship. The discussion on educational processes suggests that pre-discipleship may best be conducted with seekers through dialogue in an experiential, participatory, interactive, and communal context to enhance proper conversion and discipleship.

Pre-discipleship is thus a valid way of teaching the story of Christ to willing seekers. Although not every seeker is active in searching out truth, a significant number do want to study the basics of the faith before making any commitment. This leads to the need for a pre-discipleship curriculum, which is the focus of the following chapter.

CHAPTER NINE:

THE CONTENTS OF PRE-DISCIPLESHIP

If we are to practice pre-discipleship today, courses need to be developed with content that will provide people who have some or no knowledge of Christianity with the foundation to decide to follow Jesus. A curriculum for pre-discipleship is needed that is not so long that people lose their commitment to study and not so short that there is inadequate information for seekers to make a commitment to Jesus. What should be the contents of such a pre-discipleship curriculum? The Bible itself is the best model and source of theologically sound material. The following identifies and examines the basic topics for effective pre-discipleship classes: the person of God, the Bible, Jesus Christ, the love of God, forgiveness, and the gospel.

THE PERSON OF GOD

A pre-discipleship curriculum needs to begin with God because the course must be theocentric rather than anthropocentric. The Bible itself begins with God. *"In the beginning God created the heavens and the earth"* (Genesis 1:1) This is the Creator that the Israelites were to know. *"You were shown these things so that you might know that the LORD is God; besides him there is no other"* (Deuteronomy 4:35). Nor was the reality of knowing God exclusive to the Israelites. The prophet Isaiah writes, *"Do you not know? Have you not heard? The LORD is the everlasting God, the Creator of the ends of the earth. He will not grow tired or weary, and his understanding no one can fathom"* (Isaiah 40:28).

When the apostle Paul began a dialogue with pagan people in the meeting of the Areopagus in Athens, he began with God.

> The God who made the world and everything in it is the Lord of heaven and earth and does not live in temples built by hands. And he is not served by human hands, as if he needed anything, because he himself gives all men life and breath and everything else. From one man he made every nation of men, that they should inhabit the whole earth; and he determined the times set for them and the exact places where they should live. God did this so that men would seek him and perhaps reach out for him and find him, though he is not far from each one of us. (Acts 17:24-27)

Beginning with God still has power today, as demonstrated by Rick Warren's pre-discipleship curriculum *The Purpose Driven Life*. He writes, "It's not about you. The purpose of your life is far greater than your own personal fulfillment, your peace of mind, or even your happiness. It's far greater than your family, your career, or even your wildest dreams and ambitions. If you want to know why you were placed on this planet, you must begin with God."[230] All pre-discipleship curricula must begin with God.

THE PERSON OF GOD

Next, pre-discipleship curriculum should teach the word of God so a seeker is familiar with the validity and contents of Scripture and has a good understanding of the law of God. The majority of those in the New Testament who came to believe in Christ had a high regard for the Scriptures when they believed. In Jesus' day, knowledge of the Law and the Prophets prepared people to accept Jesus' claims. Jesus told the

---

[230] Rick Warren, *The Purpose-Driven Life* (Grand Rapids, MI: Zondervan, 2002), 17.

Jews who wanted to killed Him, *"You diligently study the Scriptures because you think that by them you possess eternal life. These are the Scriptures that testify about me, yet you refuse to come to me to have life"* (John 5:39-40).

The experience of the Apostle Paul and Barnabas in Pisidian Antioch shows the importance of the word of God in the New Testament church. Paul used the Scriptures to teach about Jesus to the Jews and the God-fearing Gentiles in the synagogue. When a large crowd wanted to hear more, some of the Jews were jealous and critical. Paul and Barnabas answered saying, *"We had to speak the word of God to you first. Since you reject it and do not consider yourselves worthy of eternal life, we now turn to the Gentiles. For this is what the Lord has commanded us: 'I have made you a light for the Gentiles, that you may bring salvation to the ends of the earth'"* (Acts 13:46-47). The Gentiles, however, responded with respect for the word of God. *"When the Gentiles heard this, they were glad and honored the word of the Lord; and all who were appointed for eternal life believed"* (Acts 13:48).

A pre-discipleship curriculum needs to help seekers gain a respect for and understanding of the word of God as the authority for all life and practice. The Bible contains a number of truths about Scripture that are important for seekers to know. Seekers must understand that *"all Scripture is God-breathed and is useful for teaching, rebuking, correcting and training in righteousness"* (2 Timothy 3:16). They must know that the Creator of the universe has revealed himself through Holy Scripture. They need to be familiar with the Bible—Old and New Testament. They need to know the law of God in order to understand their sinful status before God and need of his mercy and grace.

Seekers must ultimately be exposed to the word of God by hearing it. Jeremiah writes to the Jews, *"Hear the word of the LORD, O house of Jacob, all you clans of the house of Israel"* (Jeremiah 2:4). God also wanted those who are not his people to listen to his word. *"Consequently, faith comes from hearing the message, and the message is heard through the word of Christ"* (Romans 10:17).

The word of God must also be understood as God's law so that people can understand what sin is in the eyes of God. The psalmist writes, *"All your words are true; all your righteous laws are eternal"* (Psalm 119:160). The law reveals to people their sin and guilt before the Holy God. The law was given to show that all are lawbreakers. *"For whoever keeps the whole law and yet stumbles at just one point is guilty of breaking all of it"* (James 2:10). Only when sinners understand their sinfulness before God can they then realize their need for God's mercy and grace. The Apostle Paul said that *"the law was put in charge to lead us to Christ"* (Galatians 3:24).

Biblical scholars support the important role played by the Bible and law of God in evangelistic outreach, and by extension in a pre-discipleship curriculum. Seekers may or may not yet have accepted the Bible as an authority in their spiritual journey, but it is important for them to understand that those who follow Jesus do. J. I. Packer explains what needs to be understood about the authority of the Bible:

> Since the books were written, not to mystify, but to be understood, and since their divine Inspirer is himself present to be their interpreter, we may expect their meaning and bearing to make itself clear to us from within, as the messages of other books do, if only we attend expectantly. Then the biblical message must be allowed to confirm or correct the Church's traditions and assumptions on the one hand and our roving individual speculations on the other. It is in these terms that the authority of the Bible should be understood.[231]

Trevor McIlwain saw the law as a means in which God prepares the sinner for the gospel.

> While people are ignorant of the perfect righteousness of God, they will endeavour to save themselves through their own imperfect righteousness. Paul said

---

[231] J.I. Packer, D. Clines, F.F. Bruce, L.C. Allen, A.E. Cundall, and D. Guthrie, *Introduction to the Bible* (London: Scripture Union, 1978), 8.

of his own countrymen, *"... For they being ignorant of God's righteousness, and going about to establish their own righteousness, have not submitted themselves unto the righteousness of God"* (Romans 10:3). If a person is ignorant of the righteousness of God, then he will go about trying to establish his own righteousness. Once he sees the holiness and righteousness of God as revealed by the Law, however, he will completely abandon any trust in his own goodness as a basis for acceptance by God.[232]

Ray Comfort also emphasized the significance of the law in preparation for the gospel message. He writes, "If we are serious about reaching this world for God, we must return to the biblical principle of evangelism and use the Law of God."[233] The teaching of the word of God must ultimately reveal the Law of God. A pre-discipleship curriculum that introduces seekers to the word of God that contains the Law of God will prepare them to receive the mercy and grace of God.

THE SON OF GOD

The focus in Scripture on Jesus as the Messiah indicates that a similar focus would be important in any pre-discipleship curriculum intended to introduce a seeker to Christianity. The Old Testament pointed to a coming Messiah, the Anointed One. The psalmist predicted in reference to Zion, *"Here I will make a horn grow for David and set up a lamp for my anointed one"* (Psalm 132:17). The prophet Micah wrote, *"But you, Bethlehem Ephrathah, though you are small among the clans of Judah, out of you will come for me one who will be ruler over Israel, whose origins are from of old, from ancient times"* (Micah 5:2).

The New Testament is all about the Messiah and his impact in the world. Peter acknowledged Jesus as the Messiah, saying, *"You are the*

---

[232] Trevor McIlwain, *Firm Foundations: Creations to Christ* (Sanford, FL: New Tribes Mission, 1993), 28.

[233] Comfort, 48.

Christ, the Son of the living God" (Matthew 16:16). When the Ethiopian eunuch asked Philip to explain the meaning of a passage from Isaiah, Philip *"began with that very passage of Scripture and told him the good news about Jesus"* (Acts 8:35). The Apostle Paul writes, *"For I resolved to know nothing while I was with you except Jesus Christ and him crucified"* (1 Corinthians 2:2).

The birth, life, death, resurrection, claims, and teachings of Jesus must be at the core of any pre-discipleship curriculum. John C. Chapman writes:

> Whenever we take people through Scripture to show them the gospel—whether we are engaging in personal evangelism or speaking in groups large or small—what we must take care to do is to preach God's gospel. God's gospel is about Jesus—the historical/contemporary Jesus, the Jesus who died and rose again taking the punishment we deserved for our sins, the Jesus who is LORD, King in the Kingdom of Heaven.[234]

THE LOVE OF GOD

The emphasis in the New Testament on the importance of the message of love in Christianity indicates that Christian teachings on love would be an important part of any pre-discipleship curriculum. The Apostle Paul writes, *"But God demonstrates his own love for us in this: While we were still sinners, Christ died for us"* (Romans 5:8). Central to the teaching of Jesus is love, which identifies a disciple of Jesus. Jesus said, *"By this all men will know that you are my disciples, if you love one another"* (John 13:35). The Apostle John also understood love as central to Christianity when he writes, *"Dear friends, let us love one another, for love comes from God. Everyone who loves has been born*

---

[234] John C. Chapman, *Know and Tell the Gospel* (Colorado Springs, CO: NavPress, 1985), 22.

of God and knows God. Whoever does not love does not know God, because God is love" (1 John 4:7-8).

A person who studies Christianity without understanding the love behind it only gains information. But when people begin to understand the Christian faith in the context of love, they begin to grasp the emotive and social aspects of the Christian faith meant to be lived out in community. Bernard Brady writes, "It is fundamental to Christian teaching that God is love and Christians ought to love God and love their neighbors."[235]

THE FORGIVENESS OF GOD

Forgiveness is a progressive theme throughout the Scriptures, which suggests that the forgiveness of God is a key truth and teaching to include in a pre-discipleship curriculum. LeRon Shults writes about dominance of forgiveness and grace in Scripture:

> In both the Hebrew Bible and the New Testament we can trace a trajectory in the development of the understanding of God: in light of the revelation of Jesus Christ in the power of the Holy Spirit, the ultimate statement is that God *is* love. Divine justice is not opposed to divine mercy, but is encompassed within and fulfilled by it. I suggest that the over-arching meaning of forgiveness in Scripture is manifesting and sharing grace.[236]

The Old Testament law demanded that when a sin was committed an offering be made in the form of an animal sacrifice so that *"the priest will make atonement for them, and they will be forgiven"* (Leviticus 4:20). Receiving forgiveness from God for sin and forgiving

---

[235] Bernard V. Brady, *Christian Love: How Christians Through the Ages Have Understood Love* (Washington, DC: Georgetown University Press, 2003), 52.
[236] F. LeRon Shults and Steven J. Sandage, *The Faces of Forgiveness: Searching for Wholeness and Salvation* (Grand Rapids, MI: Baker Academic, 2003), 125.

others for their sins is central to the teachings of Jesus in the New Testament. Peter told the people in Jerusalem, *"Repent and be baptized, every one of you, in the name of Jesus Christ for the forgiveness of your sins"* (Acts 2:38). The Apostle John writes, *"If we confess our sins, he is faithful and just and will forgive us our sins and purify us from all unrighteousness"* (1 John 1:9).

Forgiveness taught in the Scriptures is not limited to God forgiving men and women, but includes men and women forgiving one another. When he taught the disciples to pray, Jesus said, *"Forgive us our debts, as we also have forgiven our debtors"* (Matthew 6:12). He also taught, *"For if you forgive men when they sin against you, your heavenly Father will also forgive you. But if you do not forgive men their sins, your Father will not forgive your sins"* (Matthew 6:14-15). Forgiveness was a key truth in the writings of the Apostle Paul. He writes, *"Be kind and compassionate to one another, forgiving each other, just as in Christ God forgave you"* (Ephesians 4:32). It is important to include the teaching of forgiveness in any introductory curriculum to Christianity.

THE GOSPEL OF GOD

In the New Testament church, pre-discipleship prepared people to make decisions for Christ when they heard the gospel. To allow people to respond positively to Christ, a curriculum needs to conclude with the gospel. Paul wrote describing the main importance of the gospel:

> Now, brothers, I want to remind you of the gospel I preached to you, which you received and on which you have taken your stand. By this gospel you are saved, if you hold firmly to the word I preached to you. Otherwise, you have believed in vain. For what I received I passed on to you as of first importance: that Christ died for our sins according to the Scriptures, that he was buried, that he was raised on the third day according to the Scriptures. (1 Corinthians 15:1-4)

Scripture makes it clear that sharing the good news is not an option. Jesus commanded, *"Go into all the world and preach the good news to all creation"* (Mark 16:15). Paul expressed his commitment to preaching the gospel writing, *"Yet when I preach the gospel, I cannot boast, for I am compelled to preach. Woe to me if I do not preach the gospel!"* (1 Corinthians 9:16).

Scripture indicates that the kingdom, as well as the death, burial, and resurrection of Jesus Christ, is the key component of the good news. Bernard Brady, who wrote on Christian love, acknowledges that love was not the central teaching of Jesus, nor would it be accurate to say that the unifying theme of the New Testament is love. Instead Brady suggests that the central teaching of Jesus was the kingdom.

> Jesus preached and lived the Kingdom of God. His teachings and actions were a witness and a pro-clamation of the Kingdom present in his life. The authors of the New Testament understood the imper-ative to love within the context of the Kingdom, which they understood as God's present and active rule in the world.[237]

Jesus started his ministry preaching about the kingdom. He said, *"Repent, for the kingdom of heaven is near"* (Matthew 4:17). He taught about who enters the kingdom when He said, *"Blessed are the poor in spirit, for theirs is the kingdom of heaven"* (Matthew 5:3). Most of his teachings were focused on the kingdom. Not only did Jesus preach extensively about the kingdom, but his disciples also preached the good news concerning the kingdom. It was said of Philip that *"he preached the good news of the kingdom of God and the name of Jesus Christ"* (Acts 8:12). In Ephesus the Apostle Paul *"entered the synagogue and spoke boldly there for three months, arguing persuasively about the kingdom of God"* (Acts 19:8). Luke writes in his conclusion to the book of Acts concerning the Apostle Paul, *"Boldly and without*

---

[237] Brady 52 NIV.

hindrance he preached the kingdom of God and taught about the Lord Jesus Christ" (Acts 28:31). The New Testament gospel is about the coming kingdom of God that is found only through the death, burial, and resurrection of Jesus Christ.

A PRE-DISCIPLESHIP CURRICULUM

Towards the end of the twentieth century, I was inspired to develop a series of discipleship materials to be used in my church at the time. I wrestled with the reality that I could get Christians to use the discipleship material but not those who were not connected with the church. Even if a seeker walked in off the street and wanted to learn about Christianity, I did not have the adequate materials for him to study. All I had were a few tracts that would push him toward a quick decision that he may not have been ready to make.

In an attempt to fill the gap, I developed a pre-discipleship tool in 2004 called *Seven Discoveries* to introduce Christianity to those who knew nothing about the faith, but wanted to learn about it. It was intended to let them make discoveries about the Christian faith in a holistic way that appealed to the mind, emotions, and will.

The first chapter of *Seven Discoveries,* Discover God, discusses the existence of God. The book begins by addressing the question, "How do we know that God really exists?" There are many with a religious background who may not ask this question, but many atheists, agnostics, and those of secular mind would find evidence of the existence of God an important place to start. I have found that there are many with a religious background who find this topic a sound reaffirmation to why they believe in the existence of God. Then it addresses the question, "If God does exist, what kind of God are we talking about?" It is important for us to distinguish the Christian God from the concepts in other religions.

The second chapter, Discover the Word of God, addresses the question, "If God does exist, does He speak to us?" It provides evidence that allows people to conclude that the Bible is the word of God and is available to be studied and obeyed. The understanding that the Bible is the word of God establishes its authority for other teaching.

If a seeker only sees the Bible as a religious book and not the word of God, it will be difficult for them embrace the teaching from the word fully. This chapter also gives Christians a foundational understanding of why the Bible is the word of God.

The third chapter, Discover the Bible, provides an overview of the Bible that enables seekers to gain a basic understanding of it. Many seekers, as well as some Christians, do not have even minimal knowledge of the Scriptures. Some of those who have used *Seven Discoveries* felt nervous, fearful, and ignorant in attempting to read Holy Scriptures, because they thought it might be too sacred to understand. This chapter has been helpful in giving seekers a basic overview of the entire Bible.

The fourth chapter, Discover Jesus, introduces the seeker to Jesus and discusses his existence, birth, life, death, resurrection, claims, and presence. A person who wants to learn about Christianity discovers Christ. The Apostle Paul wrote, *"For I resolved to know nothing while I was with you except Jesus Christ and him crucified"* (1 Corinthians 2:2). At the heart of Christianity is Jesus Christ, and this is whom this chapter presents.

The fifth chapter, Discover Love, appeals less to the cognitive side of people and more to their emotive side. Readers looking for love are challenged to consider the statement that *"God is love"* (1 John 4:16). The question to ponder is "Can one experience true love without God?" The chapter also studies the parable of the Good Samaritan, which has been used to teach many about love.

The sixth chapter, Discover Forgiveness, addresses sin and guilt. The heart of Christianity is experiencing the forgiveness of God and understanding that a forgiven person is a forgiving person. The chapter highlights the parables of the prodigal son and the unmerciful servant, emphasizing the amazing depth of God's forgiveness.

The seventh chapter, Discover the Good News, presents the gospel. This last chapter appeals to the will and asks, "What will keep you from totally following Jesus today?" Readers will be challenged with a choice to follow or not follow Jesus. At this point of the *Seven Discoveries*, a seeker has enough information cognitively, emotionally, and volitionally to make a commitment to Jesus Christ.

In summary, it has been my experience that over half the seekers who engage in the *Seven Discoveries* make a commitment to Jesus Christ. My limited study and experience in the pre-discipleship process has taught me that it works over time and is an effective aspect of evangelism. Pre-discipleship is a practice that needs to be incorporated into our evangelism.

CHAPTER TEN:

BEATING THE THOUSAND-
TO-ONE ODDS

After filtering all this information on pre-discipleship, can it really make a difference in our evangelism? Can we really beat the thousand to one odds in making disciples? To summarize, our investigation into pre-discipleship confirms it as a significant phase of Christian conversion biblically, theologically, and historically. People come to faith in Jesus Christ through a variety of means, including pre-discipleship, an approach that appeals to the many people who prefer to make major decisions through a process of study and reflection.

A PRE-DISCIPLESHIP SUMMARY

The biblical and theological focus in earlier chapters provides a biblical basis for the theology of pre-discipleship. There is quite a lot of biblical support for pre-discipleship. It shows that discipleship was common among New Testament believers, and that the disciples of Jesus were grounded in the word of God before they began to follow him. Both Jewish and Gentile converts to Christianity in the New Testament period were shown to have gone through some type of pre-discipleship process, and pre-discipleship was shown to be a common process for teaching faith that led to conversion. Images used in the New Testament to describe conversions, such as the new birth, preparing the soil, entering the narrow gate, and counting the cost in the gospels, also support the pre-discipleship process. This affirms that the practice of pre-discipleship was prevalent and calls for the use of pre-discipleship approaches today.

The focus on evangelism showed that the concept of making disciples was absent in earlier definitions of evangelism, though it is now more present in current definitions. The practice of evangelism needs to be more fluid, patient, and sensitive to the Holy Spirit, through a pre-discipleship process. The work of the evangelist is one who brings a person from an unbelieving state into maturity in Christ. We must recognize the strengths and difficulties that occur in encounter and process evangelism, leading to an understanding that many evangelistic efforts are not as effective as the church would like to believe they are. In rethinking evangelism, we must identify effective strategies and the need for a process in which seekers study the word of God in pre-discipleship. The way we reach out to the lost needs to be personal and informative.

Our focus on conversion affirmed that cognitive, emotive, and volitional changes occur in conversion, indicating that the conversion process involves the mind, emotions, and will. A look at the models of change demonstrated that conversion is a complex process that moves the convert toward transformation. The conversion process often occurs over a period of time rather than instantaneously, which means that those organizing evangelistic efforts must consider the need that some people have to digest information. This affirms that pre-discipleship can play a significant role in the conversion journey, since it does recognize the conversion process, giving people the respect and time they need to make an informed commitment to Christ.

The focus on discipleship showed that a practical relationship exists between pre-discipleship and discipleship. The characteristics and processes that are required in disciple-making processes are similar to those needed in the pre-discipleship processes. Both discipleship and pre-discipleship function best in mentoring and accountability relationships. It is highly likely for a pre-discipleship relationship to develop into a discipleship relationship. The focus on the essence of and approaches to discipleship provided insight into the essence and approaches of pre-discipleship, such as how the teaching and learning or the mentoring relationships individually or in a group context can be applied to both. What happens in pre-discipleship naturally migrates into discipleship.

The focus on adult education affirms that pre-discipleship is a significant aspect of Christian education. The history of Christian education reveals that forms of pre-discipleship existed in church history. The theories of learning and the principles of adult religious education make a case for pre-discipleship as a reliable pedagogical approach for teaching the Christian faith. The goals of religious education confirm the need for transformation, spiritual growth, and learning in the context of Christian community, relevant to pre-discipleship. The contents of pre-discipleship may best be taught to seekers through dialogue in an experiential, participatory, interactive engagement, in the context of community.

Since we know that there must be a place for pre-discipleship in the process of evangelism, we need to implement it into our outreach. The acceptance and practice of pre-discipleship allows people to have time in the process of conversion. It may change the approach of churches in their evangelism efforts so that instead of trying to pressure people to commit to Christ, they can challenge people to consider Christ through a pre-discipleship process.

A PRE-DISCIPLESHIP SCENARIO

Our thousand to one practice says that if we attract one thousand people to our evangelistic meetings, we will statistically end up with about thirty decisions for Christ. The statistics mentioned earlier reveal that most likely just one of those thirty people will become a member of a local church. If we equate discipleship to church membership, which is rarely the case, we are only producing one disciple for every thousand or so people who attend our evangelistic efforts.

How can the prospect of pre-discipleship change the odds? When we begin to apply pre-discipleship in practical terms, the major area of change would be the way that we invite people to Christ. Imagine that we still have a thousand people at an evangelistic meeting. Just for argument's sake, let's say that half of the one thousand are already Christians. That leaves us with five hundred seekers at the meeting.

152

Remember from our statistics in earlier chapters that about five percent may be ready to receive Christ, another five percent will have nothing to do with Christ, while ninety percent will want to hear more. Instead of trying to force seekers to embrace Christ before they are ready to do so, we should encourage them to discover Christ. Let's say that only half of the unbelievers are interested in this pursuit. Out of the remaining 450 unbelievers, there will be 225 who are ready and willing to invest a few weeks into discovering Christ. My studies and experience with the *Seven Discoveries* has been that over half of those who engage in this pre-discipleship tool make a serious, well-informed commitment to Christ. That means at least 113 people out of a thousand will make a commitment to Christ. This will be one more than one fifth of all the non-believers at an evangelistic event engaging in a pre-discipleship process.

This pre-discipleship process can be practiced individually, in a one-on-one context, or in a group setting. Even on an individual basis, there is still a need for mentoring relationships with accountability. Seekers who have chosen to be in a mentoring pre-discipleship relationship are already motivated to learn and have given their mentors the permission to take them to any level of spiritual depth the mentor deems acceptable. The pre-discipleship relationship naturally carries over into a discipleship relationship. The making of disciples has begun.

If we were to take three to ten percent of those who make decisions for Christ and become church members a year later, and apply it to this scenario, we will end up with four to eleven people out of a thousand who will become church members. In the worse case scenario, this will be four times more productive than our current practice of evangelism. However, due to the factor that the pre-discipleship relationship leads to a discipleship relationship, the follow-up that was so important to many evangelistic efforts becomes a natural byproduct. Another factor is that the seeker's engagement with pre-discipleship results in a commitment to Christ that is more informed, considered, and permanent. My experience has shown me that the majority of those who engage in a pre-discipleship processes before coming to Christ continue on as disciples of Christ.

Let's say that only half of those commitments continue on to be disciples of Jesus. That means about 56 out of the 113 continue on as disciples. Conservatively speaking, through the pre-discipleship process we have reduced the odds of making disciples from the odds of a thousand to one to the odds of eighteen to one. It would not surprise me if the odds are really closer ten to one using the pre-discipleship process. The bottom line with this scenario is for us to understand how we can be effective in making disciples in evangelism using the pre-discipleship process.

A PRE-DISCIPLESHIP REALITY

The practice of pre-discipleship has been in place since the dawn of the New Testament. Starting with Bet Sefer in the days of Jesus to the God-fearers in the book of Acts, from the catechumenate of the early church to the Sunday schools of the Methodist church, we have seen the development of pre-discipleship. The emergence of pre-discipleship tools such as Trevor McIlwain's *Firm Foundations*, John Cross' *The Stranger on the Road to Emmaus*, Nicky Gumbel's *Alpha Course* in recent history has confirmed that that pre-discipleship is a tested practice.

As mentioned previously, my struggle with a lack of pre-discipleship tools has led me to develop the *Seven Discoveries*. The book was developed to introduce Christianity to seekers. Over the years, I have met many who are seeking Christ, but are not yet ready to commit to Christ. The general response to these seekers from Christians has been a persistent hounding to believe until the person finally says the prayer and professes Christ. We need a better way of bringing seekers who are not ready for commitment to the faith. This was the reason that the *Seven Discoveries* came to be.

When the Buddhist family (father, mother, teenage son, and teenage daughter) who began attending our church politely refused the gospel when it was first presented to them, I came to understand that their refusal of the gospel was not a rejection of the gospel. Christians tend to put people in high-pressure, do-or-die situations when it does not have to be the case. As indicated earlier, most people will not make a commitment to Christ at a first time, all or nothing presentation of the gospel. Genuine seekers of the faith will take time to observe, study, digest, reflect, ask, and engage with the word of God before any serious commitment of faith is made. The parents from the Buddhist family were willing to spend seven weeks to study the *Seven Discoveries*. This meant that they were willing to learn more about Christianity and engage in a learning relationship with a believer.

The last discovery of the *Seven Discoveries* is the Good News. This is the chapter that, after laying a strong foundation, has a clear presentation of the gospel. When the Buddhist couple was challenged by the gospel again to make a commitment to Christ, the Buddhist man in the family said, "We understand now what it means to be a Christian. We want to be Christians." The couple was eventually baptized and are now active disciples of Christ in the church. My excitement was hearing this man share his testimony in a foreign country on a mission's trip.

The pre-discipleship process must never again be forgotten in our evangelism because it is biblical and it works. I used the *Seven Discoveries* because it assumes that the seekers know nothing about Christianity and it only takes a commitment of seven weeks. I use it because it is the tool that the Lord has given me and over half of the seekers who read it make a commitment to Christ. I am biased on the matter. However, it will not be a tool that will touch everyone. Other pre-discipleship tools like *Alpha*, *The Stranger on the Road to Emmaus*, and *Firm Foundations* have been effectively used in the making of many disciples for the kingdom. Pre-discipleship is not a new theory, but a present, growing reality in our churches.

A PRE-DISCIPLESHIP CHALLENGE

In conclusion, if the Christian church is serious about making disciples of all nations, it must embrace transformation as a process that takes time for many. Jimmy Long makes a case for such a process:

> Christians in the past treated the spiritual journey like
> a hundred-yard dash. The one who pursued a strategy

of doing the right things, such as Bible study, prayer, reading Christian literature, attending church services, participating in a small group, and continued doing all these things at the same pace throughout life would complete the race a mature Christian. Anyone who stumbled along the way would try to correct by doing even more of the above activities. This strategy just does not work any more, if it ever did. It is based on doing (certain activities) versus being. It is based on external activities, not internal transformation. It is also based on a linear view of sanctification that presupposes an ever-upward growth pattern moving from immaturity to maturity with little or no deviation from the norm.[238]

The church has witnessed many failed efforts in trying to bring people into the kingdom of God. Today's churches have become institutionalized and organized in such a way that attempts to make disciples are often mechanical and impersonal. Discipleship author Bill Hull pointed out, "The modern church is more mired in institutionalism than its first-century counterpart. Whereas the early Christian resisted change because he experienced a vibrant, caring environment, today many resist expansion because it threatens their power base."[239]

Christians feel powerless to stem the tidal wave of ineffectiveness in disciple-making, such as the shift away from away from discipleship practices of the first century. As well, ministry often end up being more politically-driven than theologically-driven. Hull describes being "haunted" by the impact of institutionalism.

"Something is wrong," I said. "It has been tormenting me for several years. All the formulas, strategic planning, mission statements and visionary sermons are not making disciples." Indeed, I was haunted by

---

[238] Long, 176.
[239] Hull 91.

it. Where was the personal transformation after all the effort we put into weekend services, Bible studies, small groups, and outreach events? We were stuck in the same rut that so many churches find themselves in—religious activity without real transformation.[240]

After wrestling with the issue of discipleship as a pastor, Hull concluded that

> True, there were many in the church who did not make this commitment to a structured plan of discipleship. I recognize now that discipleship is a way of life, not a program. It is about community and relationships and an environment of grace. So those who did not "choose the life" were not to be devalued. As their pastor I was called to love them as well. Part of the transformation in our church included extending and receiving this kind of acceptance.[241]

The frustration that those like Hull express about the disciple-making process indicates that the church has thought little about the disciple-making process among the lost. If transformation is the key to effective disciple-making, it is also the key to evangelism.

Transformation, not church attendance, is the desired result of evangelism. Yet Christians often settle for a sinner's prayer, regular attendance at church, and a small change in habit as substitutes for transformation. Gordon Smith reminds the Christian community that transformation is "the goal of all of the church's life and thus of theological reflection."[242]

Evangelism that leads to transformation takes time and patience. Biblical evangelism includes some form of pre-discipleship, a form of

---

[240] Bill Hull, "It's Just Not Working," *Leadership,* Summer 2005, 26.
[241] Ibid, 28.
[242] Gordon T. Smith, 20.

process evangelism. This, however, does not mean there is no place for encounter evangelism. A synergy must exist between encounter evangelism and process evangelism that acknowledges the time and energy it takes to bring a person to Christ. James Jauncey testifies,

> My own experience has been that it takes anywhere from six months to two years before a significant decision can be expected. Not all of this time is required to gain the necessary understanding of the person. Much of it will be necessary for the development of rapport and belongingness ... Just button-holing a stranger, witnessing to him and pressing for a decision will likely do more harm than good. Most responsible people react negatively and often quite violently to this kind of assault. It shows a fundamental lack of respect for human dignity and personality.[243]

Yet there are those in the Christian community who seem more concerned about church attendance than transformation. We live in a world where people come to church for various reasons. Some attend church to worship God. Others come out of habit and routine. Some genuinely come seeking truth. The Buddhist man mentioned earlier wanted something more. When he first heard the gospel, he was still content with being a Buddhist. However, after a series of studies in *Seven Discoveries*, the Buddhist man became a Christian and was baptized. Many like this Buddhist seeker need to go through a pre-discipleship process before they can follow Jesus.

The need for pre-discipleship is evident. Making disciples of all nations must include this pre-discipleship process, since it leads to transformation and is biblical and effective in the process of conversion. It is conceivable for people to come to Christ through a

---

[243] James H. Jauncey, *Psychology for Successful Evangelism* (Chicago: Moody Press, 1973), 122–123.

matrix of pre-discipleship applications involving relationships, account-ability, spiritual disciplines, and ministry. Leonard Sweet writes,

> The arks of modern civilization list badly. Our sundered society, buckling morality, criminal depravity have done more than just threaten to submerge modern civilization and modern culture. Like the Titanic, the modern world has taken on water and is sinking fast ... It's time to build new arks—or as Jesus would say, create "fresh wineskins."[244]

In the past, the efforts put into evangelistic-type meetings left little lasting impact. It is time to hold evangelistic meetings that lead to pre-discipleship processes that cooperate with the Holy Spirit and lead to transforming results. It is time to put new wine in new wineskins in today's evangelistic efforts. It is time for the transforming process of pre-discipleship.

---

[244] Sweet, 23.

APPENDIX

STAGES OF SPIRITUAL DEVELOPMENT

	FOWLER	LOEVINGER	HELMINIAK	PROCHASKA
Ages of Development	**Faith Development**	**Ego Development**	**Spiritual Development**	**Transtheoretical Theory of Change**
Infancy (1-2)	Pre-stage: Undifferentiated Faith	Pre-social		Precontemplative Stage
Early Childhood (2-6)	Intuitive-Projective	Symbiotic Stage		
		Impulsive Stage		
Childhood (7-12)	Mythical-Literal	Self-Protective Stage		
Adolescence (13-21)	Synthetic-Conventional	Conformist Stage	Conformist Stage	Contemplative Stage
	Transition	Self-Aware Level	Conscientious Conformist Stage	Preparation Stage
Young Adulthood	Individual-Reflective	Conscientious Stage / Individualist Level	Conscientious Stage	Action Stage
Adulthood (35-60)	Conjunctive	Autonomous Stage	Compassionate Stage	Maintenance Stage
Maturity (60+)	Universalizing	Integrated Stage	Cosmic Stage	

Bibliography

Abraham, William J. *The Logic of Evangelism.* Grand Rapids, MI: Wm. B. Eerdmans Publishing, 1989, reprint 1996.

Aldrich, Joseph C. *Life-Style Evangelism: Crossing Traditional Boundaries to Reach the Unbelieving World.* Portland, OR: Multnomah Press, 1981.

Amsterdam 2000. *The Mission of an Evangelist: Amsterdam 2000.* Minneapolis, MN: World Wide Publications, 2001.

Anthony, Michael J., ed. *Introducing Christian Education: Foundations for the Twenty-first Century.* Grand Rapids, MI: Baker Academic, 2001.

Arn, Win, and Charles Arn. *The Master's Plan for Making Disciples: How Every Christian Can Be an Effective Witness Through an Enabling Church; Church Action Kit.* Pasadena, CA: Church Growth Press, 1982.

Arndt, William F. *Luke.* St. Louis: Concordia Publishing House, 1956. Reprint in Concordia Classic Commentary Series. St. Louis: Concordia Publishing House, 1986.

Atwood, Margaret. *Bluebeard's Egg.* Toronto: McClelland and Stewart, 1984.

Aukema Cieslukowski, Corrie M., and Elmer M. Colyer. "Wesley's Trinitarian Ordo Salutis." *Reformation and Revival* 14 (2005): 105–131.

Baker, Charles F. *Understanding the Book of Acts.* Grand Rapids, MI: Grace Bible College Publications, 1981.

Bandura, Albert. "Modeling Theory" in *Learning Systems, Models, and Theories.* Edited by W. S. Sahakian, 2d edition. Chicago: Rand McNally, 1976.

Barnhart, Joe Edward, and Mary Ann Barnhart. *The New Birth: A Naturalistic View of Religious Conversion.* Macon, GA: Mercer University Press, 1981.

Baxter, J. Sidlow. *Baxter's Explore the Book.* Grand Rapids, MI: Zondervan Publishing House, 1981.

Beasley-Murray, G. R. *Baptism in the New Testament.* Grand Rapids, MI: Wm. B. Eerdmans Publishing, 1962.

Benedict, Daniel T., and Craig Kennet Miller. *Contemporary Worship for the 21st Century: Worship or Evangelism?* Nashville: Discipleship Resources, 1994, reprint 2001.

Black, Robert Allen. "The Conversion Stories in the Acts of the Apostles." PhD diss., Candler School of Theology, Emory University, 1986.

Boice, James Montgomery. *Acts: An Expositional Commentary.* Grand Rapids, MI: Baker Books, 1997.

Bowen, John P. *Evangelism for "Normal" People: Good News for Those Looking for a Fresh Approach.* Minneapolis, MN: Augsburg Fortress, 2002.

Bradley, Robert I. *The Roman Catechism in the Catechetical Tradition of the Church: The Structure of the Roman Catechism as Illustrative of the "Classic Catechesis".* Lanham, MD: University Press of America, 1990.

Brady, Bernard V. *Christian Love: How Christians Through the Ages Have Understood Love.* Washington, DC: Georgetown University Press, 2003.

Brestin, Dee. *Finders Keepers: Introducing Your Friends to Christ and Helping Them Grow.* Wheaton, IL: Harold Shaw Publishers, 1983.

Bruce, Frederick F. *The Book of the Acts.* Rev. ed. The New International Commentary on the New Testament. Grand Rapids, MI: Wm. B. Eerdmans Publishing, 1988.

BIBLIOGRAPHY

Burgess, Harold W. *Models of Religious Education: Theory and Practice in Historical and Contemporary Perspective.* Nappanee, IN: Evangel Publishing House, 2001.

Calvin, John. *The Institutes of Christian Religion.* Edited by Tony Lane and Hilary Osborne. Grand Rapids, MI: Baker Book House, 1987.

Chapman, John C. *Know and Tell the Gospel.* Colorado Springs, CO: NavPress, 1985.

Clinebell, Howard John. *Growth Groups: Marriage and Family Enrichment, Creative Singlehood, Human Liberation, Youth Work, Social Change.* Nashville: Abingdon, 1977.

Cloud, Henry and John Townsend. *Making Small Groups Work.* Grand Rapids, MI: Zondervan, 2003.

Coleman, Robert E. *The Master Plan of Evangelism.* Old Tappan, NJ: Fleming H. Revell, 1973.

————. *"Nothing to Do but to Save Souls": John Wesley's Charge to His Preachers.* Grand Rapids, MI: Francis Asbury Press, 1990.

Comfort, Ray. *Hell's Best Kept Secret.* New Kensington, PA: Whitaker House, 1989.

Comiskey, Joel. *"Cell Church Solutions,"* photocopy of manuscript by author, submitted to CCS Publishing, September 13, 2004.

Conn, Walter. *Christian Conversion: A Developmental Interpretation of Autonomy and Surrender.* New York: Paulist Press, 1986.

Coppedge, Allan. *The Biblical Principles of Discipleship.* Grand Rapids, MI: Francis Asbury Press, 1989.

Cross, John R. *And Beginning with Moses: Teaching Those Who Know Little or Nothing about the Bible.* Olds, AB: Goodseed International, 2002.

————. *The Stranger on the Road to Emmaus Workbook.* Durham, ON: Goodseed International, 2000.

Cross, K. Patricia. *Adults as Learners: Increasing Participation and Facilitating Learning.* San Francisco: Jossey-Bass Publishers, 1981.

Danby, Herbert, trans. *The Mishnah.* Oxford: Oxford University Press, 1977.

De Blank, Joost. *This Is Conversion.* London: Hodder and Stoughton, 1957, reprint 1961.

Deen, Edith. *All of the Women of the Bible.* New York: Harper & Row Publishers, 1955.

Dickinson, Gary. *Teaching Adults: A Handbook for Instructors.* Toronto, ON: New Press, 1973.

Donahue, Bill. *The Willow Creek Guide to Leading Life-Changing Small Groups.* Grand Rapids, MI: Zondervan Publishing House, 1996.

Eichhorn, David Max, ed. *Conversion to Judaism: A History and Analysis.* New York: Ktav Publishing House, 1965.

Eims, Leroy. *The Lost Art of Discipleship Making.* Grand Rapids, MI: Zondervan Publishing House, 1978.

Einstein, Stephen J., and Lydia Kukoff, eds. *Introduction to Judaism: A Course Outline.* New York: Union of American Hebrew Congregations, 1983.

Engel, James F. "Great Commission or Great Commotion?" *Eternity,* September 1977, 14.

Fisher, Richard. "The Alpha Course: Final Answer or Fatal Attraction?" *The Quarterly Journal: The Newsletter Publication of Personal Freedom Outreach* 18, no. 4. http://www.pfo.org/alpha-cr.htm (accessed September 18, 2006).

Fitzmyer, Joseph A. *The Acts of the Apostles.* The Anchor Bible. New York: Doubleday, 1998.

Foltz, Nancy T. *Handbook of Adult Religious Education.* Birmingham, AL: Religious Education Press, 1986.

Fosha, Diana. *The Transforming Power of Affect: A Model for Accelerated Change.* New York: Basic Books, 2000.

Foster, Robert D. *Essentials of Discipleship.* Colorado Springs, CO: NavPress, 1982.

Fowler, James W. *Stages of Faith: The Psychology of Human Development and the Quest for Meaning.* San Francisco: Harper Collins Publishers, 1981.

Friedeman, Matt. *Accountability Connection.* Wheaton, IL: Victor Books, 1992.

Geldenhuys, Norval. *Commentary on the Gospel of Luke.* The New International Commentary on the New Testament, edited by F. F. Bruce. Grand Rapids, MI: Wm. B. Eerdmans Publishing, 1983.

George, Carl F. *Prepare Your Church for the Future.* Grand Rapids, MI: Fleming H. Revell, 1992.

Getz, Gene A. *Sharpening the Focus of the Church.* Chicago: Moody Press, 1981.

Goldman, Israel M. *Lifelong Learning Among Jews: Adult Education in Judaism from Biblical Times to the Twentieth Century.* New York: Ktav Publishing House, 1975.

Grenz, Stanley J. *A Primer on Postmodernism.* Grand Rapids, MI: Wm. B. Eerdmans Publishing, 1996.

————. *Renewing the Center: Evangelical Theology in a Post-Theological Era.* Grand Rapids, MI: Baker Academic, 2000.

Grippin, P., and S. Peters. *Learning Theory and Learning Outcomes: The Connection.* Lanham, MD: University Press of America, 1984.

Groome, Thomas H. *Christian Religious Education: Sharing Our Story and Vision.* San Francisco: Harper & Row Publishers, 1980.

————. *Sharing Faith: A Comprehensive Approach to Religious Education and Pastoral Ministry; The Way of Shared Praxis.* San Francisco: HarperCollins Publishers, 1991.

Groothuis, Douglas. *Truth Decay: Defending Christianity Against the Challenges of Postmodernism.* Downers Grove, IL: InterVarsity Press, 2000.

Gumbel, Nicky. *Questions of Life: A Practical Introduction to the Christian Faith.* Eastbourne, UK: Kingsway Publications, 1995.

Helminiak, Daniel A. *Spiritual Development: An Interdisciplinary Study.* Chicago: Loyola University Press, 1987.

Henrichsen, Walter A. *Disciples Are Made Not Born.* Wheaton, IL: Victor Books, 1994.

Henry, Carl F. H. *Evangelicals at the Brink of Crisis: Significance of the World Congress on Evangelism.* Waco, TX: Word Books, 1967.

Heydt, Henry J. *Studies in Jewish Evangelism.* New York: American Board of Missions to the Jews, 1951.

Hiebert, D. Edmond. *The Epistle of James: Tests of a Living Faith.* Chicago: Moody Press, 1979.

Hoenig, Sidney B. *Conversion During The Talmudic Period, in Conversion To Judaism: A History and Analysis.* Edited by David Max Eichhorn. New York: Ktav Publishing House, Inc., 1965.

Hull, Bill. *The Disciple-Making Church.* Grand Rapids, MI: Fleming H. Revell, 1994.

Hunt, Dave, and T. A. McMahon. *America: The Sorcerer's New Apprentice.* Eugene, OR: Harvest House Publishers, 1988.

Hunt, Stephen. *Anyone for Alpha?: Inside a Leading Evangelising Initiative.* London: Darton, Longman and Todd, 2001.

Hutchcraft, Ron. *Living Peacefully in a Stressful World: A Strategy for Replacing Stress with Peace.* Grand Rapids, MI: Discovery House Publishers, 2000.

Hybels, Bill. *Just Walk Across the Room: Simple Steps Pointing People to Faith.* Grand Rapids, MI: Zondervan Publishing House, 2006.

James, William. *The Varieties of Religious Experience: A Study in Human Nature.* New York: Vintage Books, 1990.

Jamieson, Robert, Andrew Fausset, and David Brown. "The Jamieson, Fausset, and Brown Commentary." In *The Bethany Parallel Commentary on the New Testament.* Minneapolis, MN: Bethany House Publishers, 1983.

Jarvis, Peter. *Adult Learning in the Social Context.* London: Croom Helm, 1987.

Jauncey, James H. *Psychology for Successful Evangelism.* Chicago: Moody Press, 1973.

Johnson, Ben Campbell. *Rethinking Evangelism: A Theological Approach.* Philadelphia: Westminster Press, 1987.

Johnson, Cedric B., and H. Newton Malony. *Christian Conversion: Biblical and Psychological Perspectives.* Grand Rapids, MI: Zondervan Publishing House, 1982.

Karssen, Gien. *Her Name Is Woman.* Colorado Springs, CO: NavPress, 1976.

Kasdorf, Hans. *Christian Conversion in Context.* Kitchener, ON: Herald Press, 1980.

Keener, Craig S. *A Commentary on the Gospel of Matthew.* Grand Rapids, MI: Wm. B. Eerdmans Publishing, 1999.

Kent, Homer A. Jr. *Jerusalem to Rome: Studies in the Book of Acts.* Winona Lake, IN: BMH Books, 1972.

Kittel, Gerhard, ed. *Theological Dictionary of the New Testament.* Translated by Geoffrey W. Bromiley. Grand Rapids, MI: Wm. B. Eerdmans Publishing, 1978.

Knowles, Malcolm S. *The Modern Practice of Adult Education: From Pedagogy to Andragogy.* 2nd ed. New York: Cambridge Books, 1980.

Knox, Alan B. *Helping Adults Learn.* San Francisco: Jossey-Bass Publishers, 1990.

Kuhne, Gary W. *The Dynamics of Discipleship Training: Being and Producing Spiritual Leaders.* Grand Rapids, MI: Zondervan Publishing House, 1981.

Kumar, Steve. *Christianity for Skeptics: An Understandable Examination of Christian Belief.* Peabody, MA: Hendrickson Publishers, 2000.

Leete, Frederick D. "The Problems of Evangelism." *Methodist Review* 112 (September 1929): 757–763.

LeFever, Marlene D. *Creative Teaching Methods.* Weston, ON: David C. Cook Publishing, 1985.

————. *Learning Styles: Reaching Everyone God Gave You to Teach.* Paris, ON: David C. Cook Publishing, 1995.

Loevinger, Jane. *Ego Development: Conceptions and Theories.* San Francisco: Jossey-Bass Publishers, 1976.

Long, Jimmy. *Generating Hope: A Strategy for Reaching the Postmodern Generation.* Downers Grove, IL: InterVarsity Press, 1997.

Lüdemann, Gerd. *Early Christianity According to the Traditions in Acts: A Commentary.* Translated by John Bowden. Minneapolis, MN: Fortress Press, 1989.

MacArthur, John Jr. *Acts 13–28.* The MacArthur New Testament Commentary. Chicago: Moody Press, 1996.

————. *The Gospel According to Jesus: What Does Jesus Mean When He Says "Follow Me"?* Grand Rapids, MI: Academic and Professional Books, Zondervan Publishing House, 1988.

————. *Matthew 1–7.* The Macarthur New Testament Commentary. Chicago: Moody Press, 1985.

Manskar, Steven W. *Accountable Discipleship: Living in God's Household.* Nashville: Discipleship Resources, 2000.

Masters, Peter. *Physician of Souls.* London: Wakeman Publishers, 1976.

McGuire, Paul. *Evangelizing the New Age: The Power of the Gospel Invades the New Age Movement.* Ann Arbor, MI: Servant Publications, 1989.

McIlwain, Trevor. *Firm Foundations: Creations to Christ.* Sanford, FL: New Tribes Mission, 1993.

McKenzie, Leon, and R. Michael Harton. *The Religious Education of Adults.* Macon, GA: Smyth & Helwys Publishing, 2002.

McLaren, Brian D. *More Ready Than You Realize.* Grand Rapids, MI: Zondervan, 2002.

Merriam, Sharan B., and Rosemary S. Caffarella. *Learning in Adulthood: A Comprehensive Guide.* 2nd ed. San Francisco: Jossey-Bass, 1999.

Miller, William R., and Stephen Rollnick. *Motivational Interviewing: Preparing People for Change.* 2nd ed. New York: Guilford Press, 2002.

Morgan, G. Campbell. *The God Who Cares.* (*Books in the Master of the Word Series*) Larry Richards, ed. Old Tappan, NJ: Fleming H. Revell, 1987.

Morgan-Wynne, John E. "References to Baptism in the Fourth Gospel." In *Baptism, the New Testament and the Church: Historical and Contemporary Studies in Honour of R. E. O. White.* Edited by Stanley E. Porter and Anthony R. Cross. Sheffield: Sheffield Academic Press, 1999.

Morris, Henry M. III. *Baptism: How Important Is It?* Denver, CO: Accent Books, 1978.

Morris, Leon. *Commentary on the Gospel of John* in The New International Commentary on the New Testament, edited by F. F. Bruce. Grand Rapids, MI: Wm. B. Eerdmans Publishing, 1971, reprint 1989.

Neighbour, Ralph W. Jr. *Where Do We Go From Here?* Houston: Touch Publications, 1990.

Nettleton, David. *Chosen to Salvation: Select Thoughts on the Doctrine of Election.* Schaumburg, IL: Regular Baptist Press, 1983.

Neusner, Jacob. *The Talmud: What It Is and What It Says.* New York: Rowman & Littlefield Publishers, 2006.

Olson, C. Gordon. *Beyond Calvinism and Arminianism: An Inductive, Mediate Theology of Salvation.* Cedar Knolls, NJ: Global Gospel Publishers, 2002.

Packer, J. I., D. Clines, F. F. Bruce, L. C. Allen, A. E. Cundall, and D. Guthrie. *Introduction to the Bible.* London: Scripture Union, 1978.

Paloutzian, Raymond F. *Invitation to the Psychology of Religion.* Glenview, IL: Scott, Foresman and Company, 1983.

Patterson, Paige. "Lifestyle Evangelism." In *Evangelism in the Twenty-First Century*, edited by Thom S. Rainer, Wheaton, IL: Harold Shaw Publishers, 1989.

Peace, Richard V. *Conversion in the New Testament: Paul and the Twelve.* Grand Rapids, MI: Wm. B. Eerdmans Publishing, 1999.

Peace, Richard. *Small Group Evangelism: A Training Program for Reaching Out with the Gospel.* Downers Grove, IL: InterVarsity Press, 1985.

Percy, Harold. *Following Jesus: First Steps on the Way.* Toronto: Anglican Book Centre, 1993.

Petersen, Jim. *Lifestyle Discipleship.* Colorado Springs, CO: NavPress, 1993.

Phillips, John. *Exploring the Pastoral Epistles: An Expository Commentary.* The John Phillips Commentary Series. Grand Rapids, MI: Kregel Publications, 2004.

Poe, Harry L. "Evangelism and Discipleship." In *Evangelism in the Twenty-First Century: The Critical Issues*, edited by Thom S. Rainer. Wheaton, IL: Harold Shaw Publishers, 1989.

Poonwassie, Deo H., and Anne Poonwassie, eds. *Fundamentals of Adult Education: Issues and Practices for Lifelong Learning.* Toronto, ON: Thompson Educational Publishing, 2001.

Price, Charles. *Matthew.* Guernsey, CI: Guernsey Press, 1998, reprint 2000.

Prochaska, James O., John C. Norcross, and Carlo C. Diclemente. *Changing for Good.* New York: Avon Books, 1994.

Robinson, J. Armitage. *Commentary on Ephesians: The Greek Text with Introduction Notes and Indexes.* Grand Rapids, MI: Kregel Publications, 1979.

Rogers, Carl R. *Freedom to Learn for the 80s.* Columbus, OH: Charles E. Merrill, 1983.

Ryle, J. C. *Warnings to the Churches.* Aylesbury, UK: BPCC Hazells, 1992.

Safrai, S., and M. Stern, eds. *The Jewish People in the First Century: Historical Geography, Political History, Social, Cultural and Religious Life and Institutions.* Vol. 2. Philadelphia: Fortress Press, 1976.

Salter, Darius. *American Evangelism: Its Theology and Practice.* Grand Rapids, MI: Baker Books, 1996.

Seymour, Jack L., ed. *Mapping Christian Education: Approaches to Congregational Learning.* Nashville: Abingdon Press, 1997.

Shults, F. LeRon, and Steven J. Sandage. *The Faces of Forgiveness: Searching for Wholeness and Salvation.* Grand Rapids, MI: Baker Academic, 2003.

Simpson, E.K., and F. F. Bruce. *Commentary on the Epistles to the Ephesians and Colossians.* Grand Rapids, MI: Wm. B. Eerdmans Publishing, 1957, reprint 1982.

Simpson, Michael L. *Permission Evangelism: When to Talk, When to Walk.* Paris, ON: NexGen, 2003.

Skinner, B. F. *About Behaviorism.* New York: Knopf, 1974.

Smith, Bailey E. *Real Evangelism.* Nashville: Word Publishing, 1999.

Smith, Gordon T. *Beginning Well: Christian Conversion and Authentic Transformation.* Downers Grove, IL: InterVarsity Press, 2001.

Stanley, Paul D., and J. Robert Clinton. *Connecting: The Mentoring Relationships You Need to Succeed in Life.* Colorado Springs: NavPress, 1992.

Stöger, Alois. *The Gospel According to St. Luke.* Vol. 2. Edited by John L. McKenzie. New York: Herder and Herder, 1969.

Sweet, Leonard. *Soul Tsunami: Sink or Swim in New Millennium Culture.* Grand Rapids: Zondervan Publishing House, 1999.

Telushkin, Joseph. *Jewish Literacy: The Most Important Things to Know About the Jewish Religion, Its People and Its History.* New York: William Morrow, 1991.

Van Capelleveen, Jan J. "Evangelism and Communications." In *One Race, One Gospel, One Task: Official Reference Volumes; Papers and Reports*, edited by Carl F. H. Henry and W. Stanley Mooneyham. Vol. 1. Minneapolis, MN: World Wide Publications, 1967.

Veith, Gene Edward Jr. *Postmodern Times: A Christian Guide to Contemporary Thought and Culture.* Wheaton, IL: Crossway Books, 1994.

Vella, Jane. *Dialogue Education at Work: A Case Book.* San Francisco: Jossey-Bass, 2004.

————. *Learning to Listen, Learning to Teach: The Power of Dialogue in Educating Adults.* San Francisco: Jossey-Bass, 2002.

Wagner, C. Peter. *Acts of the Holy Spirit.* Ventura, CA: Regal Books, 2000.

Wagner, Peter. "Who Found It?" *Eternity*, September 1977, 13–19.

Walker, Thomas. *Acts of the Apostles.* Grand Rapids, MI: Kregel Publications, 1965.

Wallis, Jim. *The Call to Conversion: Why Faith Is Always Personal but Never Private.* San Francisco: Harper & Row Publishers, 1981.

Ward, Ronald A. *Commentary on 1 and 2 Timothy and Titus.* Waco, TX: Word Books, Publisher, 1974.

Warren, Rick. *The Purpose-Driven Life: What on Earth Am I Here For?* Grand Rapids, MI: Zondervan Publishing House, 2002.

Watson, David. *Discipleship.* London: Hodder and Stoughton, 1982.

Webber, Robert E. *Ancient-Future Faith: Rethinking Evangelicalism for a Postmodern World.* Grand Rapids, MI: Baker Books, 1999.

————. *Liturgical Evangelism.* Harrisburg, PA: Morehouse Publishing, 1986.

Wilkins, Michael J. *Following the Master: Discipleship in the Steps of Jesus.* Grand Rapids, MI: Zondervan Publishing House, 1992.

Williamson, G. I. *The Shorter Catechism.* Vol. 1. Phillipsburg, NJ: Presbyterian and Reformed Publishing, 1978.

Wilson, Marvin R. *Our Father Abraham: Jewish Roots of the Christian Faith.* Grand Rapids, MI: Wm. B. Eerdmans Publishing, 1989.

Wimber, John. *The Dynamics of Spiritual Growth.* London: Hodder and Stoughton, 1990.

Winter, Richard. *Still Bored in a Culture of Entertainment: Rediscovering Passion and Wonder.* Downers Grove, IL: InterVarsity Press, 2002.

Woychuk, N. A. *An Exposition of Second Timothy: Inspirational and Practical.* Old Tappan, NJ: Fleming H. Revell, 1973.

Yeung, Danny. *Getting To Yes: The ABCs of Changing Problem Behavior.* March 2003. Department of Family and Community Medicine, University of Toronto.